Phoenicia and the Phoenicians

Phoenicia and the Phoenicians

DIMITRI BARAMKI

*Professor of Archaeology
and Curator of the Museum,
American University of Beirut*

Beirut
MCMLXI

first edition

typography by John Carswell

published by KHAYATS
92-4 Rue Bliss, Beirut, Lebanon

to
J.A.S.

in recognition of her successful efforts
in creating a deep interest
among the young men and women of Lebanon
in the cultural achievement
of their land
this book is respectfully dedicated

Contents

Plates

Text Figures

FOREWORD

The present concise account of the history and art of Phoenicia the country, and the Phoenicians the people, was written at the suggestion of some of my English-speaking friends living in Lebanon.

Ever since the appearance of Rawlinson's book on the Phoenicians in the Story of the Nations series, no book has been published in the English language for the layman on the Phoenicians, although excellent accounts have been included in such big works as the Encyclopaedia Britannica and the Encyclopaedia of Religion and Ethics. A large number of books of modest size on Phoenicia have appeared, however, in French and German.

Rawlinson's Phoenicia has been out-dated and out-stripped by the various excavations carried out in Phoenicia in such places as Ras Shamra — Ugarit by Dr. Claude Schaeffer, at Byblos by M.P. Montet and M.M. Dunand, at Sidon and in its vicinity by Dr. G. Contenau and in various other places too numerous to mention.

The work is intended for the average English-speaking layman who finds himself in Lebanon, and wishes to know more about the country than is generally provided in brief guide-books.

Although great care has been taken in the preparation of the material and its accurate presentation, this book is not intended for scholars. The writer however wishes to crave the indulgence of the reader for allowing himself to hint at his pet theory regarding the origin of the Phoenicians. The writer hopes in due course to publish a more critical treatment of this subject, corroborated by evidence, which will be presented and discussed in greater detail.

The author wishes finally to gratefully acknowledge the encouragement he received from various people in the preparation of the book. In particular, the writer wishes to thank the Emir Maurice Chéhab, Director General of Antiquities in Lebanon for permission to reproduce Plates No. 1-3 and 8 ; and to Monsieur Henry Seyrig, Director of the French Institute of Archaeology in Lebanon and Monsieur Maurice Dunand, the excavator of Byblos and Marathus for the helpful information and suggestions they invariably extended to the author from time to time. The map and the text figures were specially drawn for this publication by Mr. John Carswell.

Foreword

The section on coins in Chapter IV has been treated rather fully, because of the interest of the English-speaking residents of Lebanon in Phoenician coins. Time and again coins were brought to the present writer for identification by his friends, who pressed him to write a short account for the average layman, as the scholarly books on the subject are difficult to understand. The writer hopes that the present work will satisfy them.

Beirut, January 1961.

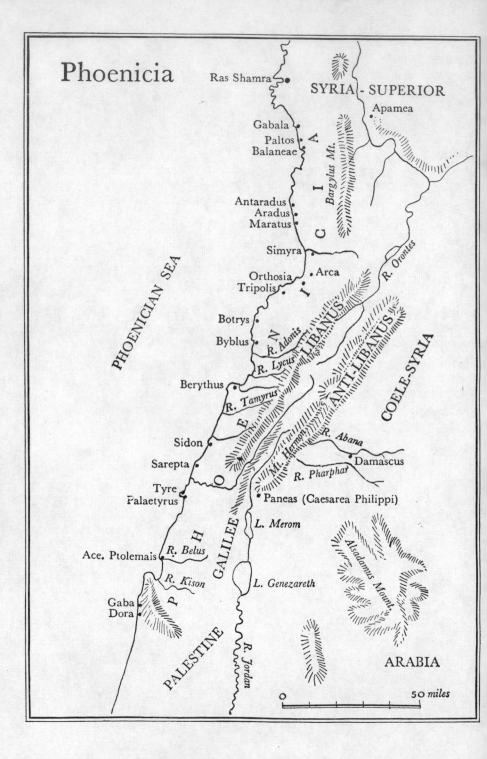

Phoenicia

Ras Shamra

SYRIA - SUPERIOR

Apamea

Gabala
Paltos
Balaneae

Bargylus Mt.

Antaradus
Aradus
Maratus

Simyra

Arca

R. Orontes

Orthosia
Tripolis

Botrys

Byblus

R. Adonis

R. Lycus

LIBANUS

ANTI-LIBANUS

COELE-SYRIA

Berythus

R. Tamyrus

Sidon

Sarepta

Tyre
Falaetyrus

R. Abana

Mt. Hermon

Damascus

R. Pharphar

Paneas (Caesarea Philippi)

L. Merom

PHOENICIAN SEA

PHOENICE

GALILEE

Alsadamus Mount.

Ace. Ptolemais

R. Belus

R. Kison

L. Genezareth

Gaba
Dora

PALESTINE

R. Jordan

ARABIA

O   50 miles

CHAPTER I
The Land

Phoenicia lies along the eastern littoral of the Mediterranean. What was called Phoenicia at various times in history varied from time to time, but during the Golden Age of Phoenicia's history, the country consisted of a narrow strip of territory bounded on the north by the mouth of the Orontes (Nahr el As) in the Amuq plain, on the east by the Jebel Nuseiriyeh mountain range and the more formidable Lebanon range to the south, and on the south by the Belus or the Kishon (modern Nahr el Muqatta').

This narrow strip of territory is traversed by the deep gorges and ravines of a large number of small, swift rivulets and streams, few of them worthy to be called rivers. The streams have cut for themselves these deep gorges through the ages, and effectively divided the country into several isolated cantons. Communication between one canton and the other was extremely difficult, if not hazardous, especially after heavy rainfall to which the area is frequently subjected. Communication is especially difficult when the snow on the mountains starts thawing early in spring; bridges were unknown in the Near East until the Roman Period.

The narrow plain lying at the foot of the Nuseiriyeh and the Lebanon Mountain ranges is washed by no less than fourteen torrential streams with deep gorges, which cannot be forded during the winter and spring and are extremely difficult to cross at any time of the year. In addition a number of less formidable smaller streams cross the plain and debouch into the sea but these can be crossed without difficulty at all times. Each of the ancient city-states of Phoenicia grew and developed in the midst of an area situated between a pair of such gorges. Thus Ras Shamra-Ugarit at the extreme north end of Phoenicia, is situated between the mouth of the Orontes and Nahr el Kabir, a small stream south of Lattaqia (ancient Laodicea). The two rivers effectively separate the territory controlled by the city, from the land of Alalakh (Tel Atchana) beyond the mouth of the Orontes in the north, and the canton of Jableh (ancient Gabala) in the south. The canton of Jableh is contained between Nahr el Kabir and Nahr Sukaz which lie respectively north and south of the city. Banias (Graeco-Roman Balanea) lies between Nahr Sukaz and Nahr Markhieh.

The famous island-port of Aradus controlled the territory between Nahr Markhieh and Nahr el Abrash. The canton of the port of Simyra comprised the area falling between Nahr el Abrash and the Eleutheros (modern Nahr el Kabir, the second river of the same modern name). Similarly all the other cities were effectively isolated from their neighbours by deep gorges; Botrys lay between Nahr el Bared and Nahr el Jauz, Byblos (Jubail) between Nahr el Jauz and the Adonis (Nahr Ibrahim), Beirut between the Lycus (Nahr el Kalb) and the Tamyrus (Nahr ed Damur), Sidon between the Asklepios (Nahr el Awwali) and the Leontes (modern Nahr el-Litani or Nahr el Qasimiyeh), Tyre between the Leontes and the promontory of the Ladders of Tyre (modern Ras el Naqurah on the Palestine frontier) and Acre between the Ladders of Tyre and the Kishon (modern Nahr el Muqatta', the Graeco-Roman Belos).

The ancient boundaries of Phoenicia are thus not coterminous with those of the modern Republic of Lebanon. On one hand the littoral between the mouths of the Orontes and the Eleutheros in the north and the plain of Acre in the south were part of Phoenicia, but at the present time the former is in Syria and the latter in Palestine; on the other hand the Lebanon Mountains and the Biqa (Coele-Syria) were not part of ancient Phoenicia.

While the Nuseiriyeh Mountains in the north rise some distance from the coast, the Lebanon range rises abruptly from the sea leaving a very small strip of cultivable land for the sustenance of the people living on the coast, between the mountains and the sea.

Anyone familiar with Greek history and the factors which helped to mould it, sees in Phoenicia a reflection of the same natural forces at work. In Lebanon, as in Greece, the coast is provided with numerous bays and coves which can be used as harbours. This, coupled with difficult overland communication, made the inhabitants of Phoenicia turn to the sea as the natural means of communicating with one another and converted the sea into a high road at an early date. Thus from the outset, the destiny

2

of the inhabitants of Phoenicia was linked with the sea, and however cramped they may have felt on land with its formidable mountain barriers and impenetrable torrential rivers, the sea with its wide expanse and its shimmering blue waters invited them to make use of it, and tap the untold hidden treasures which lay in the lands beyond. Well might they repeat with the Athenian neophytes:

"Seaward, O mystae, to the sea!"

However, the torrential unnavigable rivulets of Lebanon had a deeper and a more profound effect on the history of Phoenicia. The Tyrians, Sidonians and Arvadites may communicate by sea, but communication by sea is not of itself such a strong unifying factor as to overcome the isolationism or separatism which the mountain barriers and ravines bred in the hearts of the inhabitants of the coast. As in Greece, a country devoid of great plains but like Lebanon traversed by steep mountain chains and deep gorges of torrential streams, so in Lebanon we find that these seemingly innocent streams have acted as insurmountable barriers to political unity. One does not feel a strong political bond with a city which he can only reach by sea, no matter how completely that sea may be harnessed to serve one's needs. Thus Phoenicia remained a disunited country, each city being independent of the other, and as the economy of each was, by force of circumstances, similar to that of its neighbour, a deep sense of rivalry and jealousy arose between the various cities which went further to deepen the geographical chasm. Unity, if such it may be called, was only achieved when a foreign power dominated the entire country, and even then, the causes of isolationism and separatism were by no means eradicated, but merely muffled and left simmering and ever ready to flare out again. Many a time in the history of Phoenicia when one city revolted against a foreign power, its rival city would help the foreign power to quell the revolt. Several examples of this will be given when we come to discuss the history in detail.

The natural resources of Phoenicia were limited. The role of the population was not so much the exploitation of the resources of their country, which in area was extremely circumscribed, as the transport and rendering available the products of their various

3

neighbours to one another. However, we cannot do the Phoenicians justice if we do not mention the thorough exploitation of what meagre resources their country had. Fishing, as we shall later see, was one of the chief reasons which led to the settlement of the coast of Phoenicia long before the days of maritime trade. Fish were considered a great delicacy among the ancients and the cradle of civilization relied almost entirely on the fish caught off the Phoenician coast. The second chief product of Phoenicia was the purple dye. This was extracted from the murex shell which abounded on the coast of Phoenicia in antiquity, but which was so thoroughly exploited that it is now extinct.

Apart from these two, and the growing of cereals and vegetables in the small area at the foot of the hills, there were no other means of livelihood. The inhabitants of Phoenicia had perforce to look for other means of subsistence in other spheres. Let us now turn to the people of the country and examine the steps taken by them to augment the meagre resources of their country in order to live a healthy, contented life.

In spite of its small size, Phoenicia boasts a great diversity in its landscape, and it is one of the most picturesque countries in the world. The coast is broken by numerous inlets and coves, and possesses one of the most beautiful bays in the world, the Bay of Jounieh. Although the mountains in the hinterland do not form part of ancient Phoenicia, yet they can be seen best from Phoenicia and form a beautiful and impressive background to the picturesque coast. The Lebanon Mountains rise abruptly above the Mediterranean and lend the country a variety of rich hues. The peaks are in spotless snow most of the year, while below them the slopes form an array of mellow colours which merge one with the other into a delightful pattern; the buff colour of the soil, the grey of the outcrops of rock and the green of the luxuriant forests give a feeling of repose and contentment. It is a setting fit for artistic inspiration, which indeed was not wasted on the inhabitants of the country either in antiquity or in the present day. The variety of the landscape of Phoenicia makes of the country a museum or a gallery of geographical and geological features that the visitor can see, with one sweep of the eyes, and from several vantage points; miniature plains, miniature rivers, deep gorges and ravines flanked by forbidding and steep peaks, while here and there the

4

pleasant cool springs which gush out of the solid rock, have converted Phoenicia into one of the most pleasant of summer resorts.

CHAPTER II
The People

Amorites and Canaanites

Phoenicia, like its sister states of Syria and Palestine, was inhabited by man from the earliest times. Palaeolithic, or Old Stone Age implements have been discovered in various parts of the country. What species of man lived in Phoenicia over 180,000 years ago we do not know, but we do know that about that time Neanderthal man made his appearance in this part of the world and held sway for a very long time. By about 100,000 years ago, Neanderthal man gave place to *homo sapiens*. The struggle of species most likely took place in the Near East, and Phoenicia undoubtedly formed part of the stage of that great drama.

With the approach of the Neolithic Age (the New Stone Age), we are on surer ground. The skeletons and skulls show that the Neolithic race in Phoenicia belonged to a brachycephalic race of short stature. The population of the country during this period appears to be a Mediterranean folk, but it is not possible to ascertain their race more precisely.

About 3500 B.C. a new Semitic folk, the first of a series of waves of Semites which periodically overflowed from the over-populated, sparsely cultivated, and underwatered Syrian and Arabian deserts, burst into Egypt by way of the Red Sea and perhaps overflowed into Phoenicia. [1] These new people overcame the aboriginal inhabitants, subdued them and in process of time completely absorbed them. In Phoenicia they settled along the coast at places like Ras-Shamra and Byblos (and many other places which are awaiting the excavators' spade). These folk introduced painted and burnished pottery, burial in jars, and the use of copper. Byblos became the centre of a lumber trade, immediately upon the advent of the new folk; cedar and pine trees were felled in the adjacent Lebanon hills, rolled or carted down to Byblos, and from there towed in rafts to Egypt.

From this period, the relations of Egypt with Byblos became

[1] Their culture in Egypt is known as Gerzean.

very close, as will be discussed later, and the Phoenician city started figuring even in Egyptian mythology.

Another wave of Semites penetrated the Fertile Crescent from the desert about 2900-2800 B. C. This wave brought with it new techniques in pottery making. Two or three centuries later, the Near East saw a wave of an Armenoid race who came from the Caucasus. The line of their advance has been traced by the introduction of a new type of pottery, the so-called Khirbat el-Kerak ware, which in recent years has been retrieved by excavators in the corresponding occupation levels of the period. Sir Leonard Woolley has with some justification identified these new folk with the early Hittites. [1] They penetrated Phoenicia, Syria and Palestine as far as the Sea of Galilee and Megiddo.

However, the wave of Semites which was to hold sway over the Fertile Crescent for about 1000 years was the great Amorite invasion which occurred between 2300 and 2100 B.C. This wave apparently came to Phoenicia, Syria and Palestine and subsequently spread eastwards to Mesopotamia. It was this wave which gave the final Semitic character to the Near East. In process of time, the invaders divided themselves into two separate entities; those who settled in the hinterland continued to be called Amorites and those who settled in Phoenicia and Palestine came to be known as the Canaanites or "Lowlanders". [2]

About 1194, when the Dorians invaded Greece in large numbers, pushing the former inhabitants, the Aegeans, out of their country and forcing them to seek new homes elsewhere, the Aegeans or "People of the Sea" descended on the coast of Phoenicia and Palestine. One wave spread from the West Coast of Asia Minor inland, destroyed the Hittite Kingdom and moved south along the coast, destroying Alalakh (Tell Atchana in the Amuq plain), Ugarit (Ras Shamra), Aradus and several other cities on or near the coast in their stride. Another wave threw itself on Egypt, but they were defeated by Rameses III at the Battle of Pelusium. Rameses III, however, was powerless to throw

[1] Or Hattians, as they are now called.
[2] This was the generally accepted view among scholars, but recently some scholars claim that the name Canaan is derived from the Hurrian word "Kenaggi" which means red and is thus the equivalent of the Greek word Phoenician.

7

them back into the sea, and had to allow them to settle on the Palestine Coast. From there they spread northwards sacking Tyre and Sidon and some other less important cities. In process of time the Aegeans were assimilated by the Canaanites of Phoenicia but not without completely changing the character, culture and economy of the inhabitants.

The Aegeans

Let us now turn to the Aegeans and find out who they were, what they were, what was the level and nature of their civilization, what were their capacities and capabilities, their potentialities and possibilities. Sir Arthur Evans has discovered, during his long career as an excavator in Crete, a civilization on the Island at Knossos which goes back to the Early Bronze Age (3000-2000 B.C.). Of the history of this early period we are quite ignorant although we know something about the culture and art, especially the ceramic art, of the period. However, a palace was constructed at Knossos about 2000 BC. which was rebuilt about 1500 B.C. with great additions and embellishments. The drainage system in the second palace was superior to any subsequent system until the Roman Period. The palace walls were decorated with frescoes of a high quality. From these frescoes we learn that the women of Knossos freely mixed with the men and took part in bull fighting which, again judging by the frescoes, seems to have been the national pastime of the Minoans, as Sir Arthur Evans called the race.

The kings of Knossos must have been wealthy sovereigns to be able to spend so lavishly on their palaces. Part of their revenue came from trade as the numerous storage jars discovered in the magazines of the palace testify. Sir Arthur Evans was struck by the absence of fortifications of the palace at Knossos on the north coast, and Phaistos on the south coast, of the island. He came to the conclusion that the Kings of Knossos relied for their protection on a strong navy which controlled the Aegean Sea and its basin, and which in addition carried the merchandise from one part of the Aegean to the other, thereby bringing untold wealth to the lords of Knossos. The thalassocracy, or sea-power, of Knossos lasted for several decades.

The earlier excavations of Schliemann and others on the mainland of Greece and in the Cyclades indicated that the thalassocracy

8

of Knossos embraced the entire Aegean basin, which owed allegiance to the lords of Knossos and no doubt paid tribute to the island sovereigns.

However, a new race, the Achaeans, started infiltrating into Greece during the Second Millennium B.C. In process of time they became strong enough to shake off the Minoan yoke. By about 1400 B.C. they had become sufficiently strong to attack Crete and destroy the royal palaces at Knossos and Phaistos in the island. We do not know where the centre of the power of the Achaeans was, but palaces built by them were discovered in Tyrins, Mycenae in the Peloponnesus and Gla in Boeotia. Archaeologists starting with Petrie called their culture Mycenaean, as it was at Mycenae that Schliemann first discovered Achaean culture, and where the penetration of that culture was subsequently encountered, it was called Mycenaean, after the first place where it was discovered. Furthermore we gather from Homer's *Iliad* that the king of Mycenae held a loose political hegemony or overlordship over the rest of the Achaean kings.

The Achaeans or Mycenaeans inherited the thalassocracy of Knossos, and with their vast mercantile and war navy they extended their trading activities beyond the limits set by the Minoans. They established strong centres in Cyprus, which they controlled, and entered into trade relations with the Hittites of Asia Minor, the cities of the Phoenician coast and Egypt. They were masters not only of the Aegean but of the Eastern Mediterranean as well. Pots made in Mycenae and other Mycenaean centres were discovered all along the Phoenician coast and Egypt. Their empire seemed to have been more stable than that of Knossos and it would have been a very brave prophet who could at the time have foretold that this vast political and economic structure was to come tumbling down and bring about vast changes in the Near East.

Between 1200 and 1100 B.C. large hordes of uncivilized Indo-European barbarians started from their homes in the Delta of the Danube, (being possibly pushed by still vaster and more savage hordes coming from Central Asia), and penetrated the Aegean basin. Their large numbers and their cheaper iron weapons enabled them to vanquish the Aegeans (the Achaeans and their kindred tribes), who were armed with a limited number of the more expensive bronze weapons. The Dorians, as the newcomers were called, caused a great commotion in the Aegean basin; the inhabitants of the Aegean were no match in numbers or fighting quality for the newcomers, and vast numbers of them sought refuge from slavery or death in flight. A large wave fleeing before the Dorians moved across Asia Minor, destroyed the Hittite State of Anatolia, sacked Hattusas the capital of the Hittites, and moved south along the Phoenician coast destroying Alalakh in the Amuq plain near the mouth of the Orontes, Ras Shamra, Aradus and other Phoenician cities, in their stride as we saw. A second wave descended by sea on Egypt, which they knew well as they had previously established trade relations with that country for more than 200 years. They were met by Rameses III at Pelusium and although defeated they were allowed to settle in Palestine as we have seen. They moved up the coast destroyed Tyre, Sidon and other less important Phoenician cities and held Palestine and Phoenicia in subjection.

The Phoenicians

In process of time the Aegeans, or "People of the Sea" as the Egyptians called them in their annals, were assimilated by the inhabitants of Phoenicia and by about 1100 B.C. the fusion of the two races, the proto-Phoenician Semitic Canaanites and the Indo-European Aegeans, gave birth to a new and virile nation of seamen which quickly stepped into the gap left by the displaced Achaeans, and established a thalassocracy over the Eastern basin of the Mediterranean and the Aegean. For a period of 400 to 450 years the Phoenicians (and at this stage it is appropriate to call the inhabitants of Phoenicia, Phoenicians) held complete sway over the high seas. No ship belonging to any other nation was allowed to put to sea without being captured or sunk and its crew sold as slaves. The Phoenicians held a monopoly over the seas and over marine trade in the very centre of Dorian Greece itself as we shall see. One may ask how this new race was able to do this? According to the view of the present writer, the Phoenicians were able to accomplish this great feat, because they were descended in part from the Aegeans who had formerly lived in the Aegean basin, and who had learnt from their parents something about their ancient sagas. Travelling in small boats in those days, without maps or a compass, was a great hazard, but it is submitted that among the Phoenicians there were some who had learnt from their parents about the promontories, crags and coves of every part of Greece; they had learnt about currents, direction of prevailing wind and presence of dangerous rocks.

The Dorians, as was stated above, were uncivilized, and apart from iron weapons and tools and primitive pottery they hardly produced anything else. Phoenicia, with the culture of the vast hinterland behind her, and her own numerous products, was very conveniently situated to act as the "middle nation" between the uncivilized west and the civilized east. With the sea at their disposal, and the experience of the newly assimilated Aegeans, the Phoenicians took advantage of the situation and established trade relations with the Greek world. Trading stations or factories were established at Corinth, Thebes and elsewhere, and Phoenicia traded her products and those of her neighbours in the Fertile Crescent and Egypt for the weapons of the Dorians, and received large numbers of slaves in addition. It was some time before the Dorians were sufficiently civilized and able to barter their own products for the products of the Orient.

We thus see that the new nation was conveniently situated and adequately equipped to control marine trade, and fill the gap left by the expelled Achaeans and their kindred races. The story of Phoenicia is the story of the exploitation by the Phoenicians of the limited resources of their country. They took full advantage of every opportunity which presented itself and reaped the benefits placed at their disposal by force of circumstances and historical accidents. It is convenient now to turn to the history of the country, and trace the rise of the country from the earliest times down to the Golden Age of Phoenician expansion when it reached its climax, and follow the later fate of the country when it came under the rule of the various great powers which controlled it. It is of great interest to follow the role played by the Phoenicians under the tutelage of each of the great powers of the past, and conclude our narrative with the expulsion of the Byzantine rulers from this part of the world. In doing so, we must bear in mind the constant blood transfusions which the various nations or races injected into the Phoenicians, as it is an important factor which helped to retain the virility of the race.

CHAPTER III

The History of Phoenicia

The Stone Age

In discussing the inhabitants of Phoenicia, we mentioned that the country was occupied during the Palaeolithic Period. At that early period, man generally selected riverside terraces and plains for his abode. From the flint implements he left behind him we know that Old Stone Age Man established stations in the vicinity of Nahr el Jauz, near Batrun, Nahr Ibrahim (the ancient Adonis), Nahr el Kalb (the ancient Lycus), Beirut (Furn esh-Shubbak, Bir Hassan, the Pigeon Rocks and Nahr Beirut), Jubeil (the caves in the foothills), Khaldi, Sidon and the rock shelter at Ksar 'Akil, near Antelyas. This list of stations is not exhaustive by any means and several other stations may have been occupied at that early stage. However, it should be emphasized that the human population during the Early Stone Age was very sparse and widely scattered. It may not be too bold to assert that the animal population of the country was much larger than its human population. Man's sole occupation and chief problem was to gather enough food to sustain himself and his folk, and to defend himself against the wild animals such as lions, tigers, wolves, gorillas and others which are now extinct in the area, but with which he was then surrounded. During the early stage of the Palaeolithic Period, the period known as the Lower Palaeolithic Age, the stations were situated in open plains or riverside terraces, and in self-preservation men congregated into small communities and lived in close proximity to one another. Men hunted and fought with clumsy flint hand-axes, at first large, shapeless and blunt (Abbevillian) and later with better hand-axes more or less triangular in shape and pointed at the apex (Acheulian). The species of man responsible for this primitive culture is unknown. This stage of savagery ended about 180,000 years ago to be followed by a higher culture. During the latter period, the Fourth Ice Age (the Wurm Ice Age) started, and we find man moving from the open and riverside terraces to take shelter in large and spacious natural caves or rock shelters. About that time man learnt how to control fire and how to start it, perhaps accidentally at first, by striking two flints against each other near a twig. The discovery of fire had far-reaching conse-quences in man's culture. By its means he was able to keep warm, to scare away wild animals and to make better and handier flint tools. He discovered that by heating the flint core first, he could strike thin blades off it. The blade would flake off the core at the point of percussion, and would then be trimmed and fashioned into a serviceable tool. This epoch in man's culture is called Levallois-Mousterian and is characteristic of the Middle Palaeo-lithic Period (180,000-80,000 years ago). The species of man who was responsible for this culture is Neanderthal man but, by the end of the period, *homo-sapiens* made his appearance and Neander-thal man slowly gave way before him. It was in the Near East generally, including Phoenicia, that the struggle between the two species *homo-Neanderthalensis* and *homo-sapiens* took place; by about 80,000 years ago *homo-Neanderthalensis* had disappeared completely.

The Upper Palaeolithic Period (80,000-10,000 years ago) saw great improvements in man's culture. The tendency to reduce the size of his flint implements which at first ran concurrently with the reduction of the size of his hands, continued, and he started using wood and jaw-bones of animals as handles for his tools and weapons. His tools, instead of being limited to cores and flakes, now included greater varieties such as points on flakes, burins, gravers and scrapers. A rock-shelter with stratified occupation levels of this period was discovered at Ksar 'Akil, near Antelyas. The site has since been excavated and a large variety of Aurignacian flint implements followed by local variations of the developments of the later phases of this culture were encountered. In addition to flints, snail shells pierced with large holes were discovered; these were probably strung on a leather thong and worn as neck-laces. Although agriculture was not ushered into world history until the following Mesolithic Period, some basalt querns were dis-covered in the cave indicating that man at least started grinding wild wheat into flour at that early age.

The Post-Palaeolithic or Mesolithic Period (the Middle Stone Age) was of a very short duration, and lasted only about 2500 years. However during that relatively short period of time great advances were made in man's culture. First of all his flint tools

13

and implements were very small and dainty, graceful and elegant in shape. There were crescent-shaped flints (lunates), arrow-heads, small engravers used for carving on bone and many other varieties. The industry of the period has been characterized as microlithic on account of the minuteness of the size of the various implements produced. The period ushered agriculture into world history. Sickle-blades made of small flint blades set in the frames of jaw-bones or curved branches make their appearance for the first time. Man changed his economy and did not live only by gathering food as hitherto, but now he became a producer as well. The dog and probably other animals such as the sheep and the goat were domesticated. However, on account of his inefficient tools Mesolithic man could only cultivate a small patch of ground in front of his cave. Yet this economic revolution led to a complete and radical change in man's mode of life and culture. It led to a rapid increase in the human population of Phoenicia, created new needs, and compelled man to devise ways to meet them. With the increase of the population, the small patch of cultivable land in front of the cave was no longer adequate. Thus we find man, some time between 6000 and 5500 B.C., leaving his cave perdiodically and descending into the plain in search of larger areas for cultivation. Eventually during the Neolithic or New Stone Age, he left his cave for good and proceeded to build shelters close to the land which he culti-vated. In time the shelters increased in number and thus the first village came into existence. Man came to depend more and more on his agricultural products and less and less on the hazards of hunting, which however was not neglected. The dis-covery of a large number of fish-hooks in bone is clear evidence that fishing formed a part of man's economy during this period. The break with the past by Neolithic or New Stone Age man was just as revolutionary as the discovery of fire. The face of the earth was completely changed; numerous villages arose in Phoenicia and elsewhere, where formerly there was nothing but uncontrolled wild growth, and fields were tilled which formerly lay fallow. Neolithic huts were simple small rooms, built of lumps of mud, reinforced by straw; each hut was built over a rough stone foundation and covered with branches of trees, leaves and mud. The stones used for the foundations by the Neolithic inhabitants of Phoenicia were gathered from the river beds or from small stones that had got detached from large boulders in process of time by the action of water or heat. Quarrying was unknown. The floors of huts were covered with crushed limestone made into a paste and beaten hard into a compact mass. The tools of Neolithic man underwent great changes in order to meet his new needs. The minute implements of the Mesolithic Age were no longer adequate for extensive cultivation. Large implements re-appeared. Axes for felling small trees or for lopping branches off large trees were made; they consisted of a flint axe-head and a wooden haft or handle to which it was attached. The axe-head was made of flint or chert, more or less rectangular in shape; one end of it, the cutting edge, was sharpened to a thin blade and highly polished and the other, the end which was tied to the handle was left blunt. The handle was made of a branch and the axe-head was tied with dried leaves or dried grass to the branch between it and the knot of a twig which was purposely left in place in order to obtain a firm grip on the axe-head. Sharp-pointed hoes were made to dig furrows in the ground and attached to handles in the same manner. Small axe-heads or celts of diorite and serpentine were made and highly polished. Some of these were worn as amulets and others were used as weapons of war. Arrow-heads, spear-heads, knives, awls and various other tools were added to the repertoire of tools used by Neolithic man. Beads made of serpentine, carnelian, ivory and bone were made and worn; they were polished on pebbles gathered from river-beds.

Man's economy having changed, he had to store food for the period between harvests and for the sowing for the subsequent year. He therefore proceeded to carve stones into vessels, but his principal vessels were animal skins.

About the year 4750 B.C. Neolithic man discovered pottery. It has been suggested that the discovery of pottery was due to the accidental conflagration of a mud hut, somewhere in Iraq. It was noticed by the villagers of the time that the mud, which was of clay, hardened into an impervious substance on being subjected to intense heat. This suggested the possibility of making vessels from this plastic substance, instead of laboriously carving vessels out of limestone or diorite or using animal skins as storage vessels as hitherto. Whether this theory is based on fact or fancy, is immaterial for the purpose of this study. However, one thing is certain, Neolithic man did start making pottery in Phoenicia as we know from the excavations of Byblos and Ras Shamra, [1] about 4750 B.C. and that the earliest pots made by Neolithic man in Phoenicia and elsewhere contained straw as a binder; at the outset, the vessels were built up piece by piece, just as Neolithic man built his houses. Later Neolithic man lined the inside of wicker-work baskets and bowls, and burnt the basket, leaving a handy vessel inside. The pots were decorated with finger nail incisions to resemble the impressions of basket-work vessels.

The remains of a fishermen's village going back to the Neolithic Period were discovered at Byblos. The dead were buried below the floors of the houses. It has been suggested that some sort of belief in an after-life led Neolithic man to strive for the preservation of the bodies of his dead. This belief was further strengthened by the discovery of mud figurines in the various Neolithic occupation levels of Phoenicia. The implements used for digging by the inhabitants of Neolithic Phoenicia were not adequate for digging deep graves in which to bury their dead and secure them from wild animals. The dead were laid in pits, sometimes within a cradle of stones, with the body flexed so that the chin rested against the knee. Neolithic remains were also discovered at Ras Shamra including flint and bone implements and tools, and pottery decorated with incised patterns. No doubt, the various unexcavated sites of Phoenicia will yield further evidence of Neolithic settlements along the coast when funds permit their exploration. Neolithic flint implements were discovered on the surface of the ground at the Lycus (Nahr el Kalb) and at the Zahrani, south of Sidon.

The Bronze Age

Sometime in the Fourth Millennium B.C. copper started making its appearance. Flint implements of a higher polish and more varied forms continued in use for sometime, but about 3500 B.C. some copper weapons such as daggers started making their appearance. [2] Nevertheless flint knives and other flint implements

[1] At Ras Shamra fragments of unfired clay vases were discovered by the excavator which suggests that it may have been actual pots, accidentally fired in a conflagration, which suggested the idea of firing.

[2] The introduction of copper may have been linked with the first wave of Semitic penetration into the Fertile Crescent. This wave may also be in some way related to the introduction of Gerzean culture into Egypt.

continued in use. This was the transitional period from the age of stone to the age of bronze; it has been inappropriately called the Chalcolithic Age, although copper did not come into use till the second half of the period. However, the age is more noted for the development of architecture and for the expansion of the ceramic industry. Painted pottery makes its appearance but the chief characteristic feature of the pottery of the time is the presence of large amounts of large grits in the ware. Both at Ras Shamra and at Byblos Chalcolithic settlements were discovered. Strata IV and III at Ugarit correspond with Tell Halaf in the hinterland of Syria, and with Uruk and Jemdet Nasr in Mesopotamia. At Ras Shamra, so far, only a sounding in a restricted area reached the Chalcolithic strata, but at Byblos an extensive settlement has been exposed with no less than 1800 burials so far.

Chalcolithic houses were generally built on an apsidal plan. The foundations were of stone, but the walls were built of rectangular bricks. Timber was used extensively for roofing, either as posts or as rafters.

Pottery was moulded by hand and contained a large quantity of grits, sometimes as much as fifty per cent of the content of each pot. In the Tell el Halaf levels (Ras Shamra IV) the ware is thin and sometimes painted in red and brown. The dead were buried under the floors of houses in large jars; belief in the after-life is indicated by the presence of bowls and beakers, which no doubt contained food and drink at the time of burial. Towards the later stages of the period, pots decorated in monochrome with geometric patterns slowly replaced the polychrome painted vessels. Eventually pots of grey ware, highly burnished, bring the period to an end. The Jemdet Nasr thick pottery bridges the gap between Late Chalcolithic and Early Bronze. So far no city-walls have been discovered either at Byblos or at Ras Shamra which can be attributed to the Chalcolithic Age, but in view of the fact that city-walls were discovered at Neolithic Jericho and Chalcolithic sites elsewhere, it is possible that they may turn up in the future.

Apart from the information about the culture of the period gleaned from archaeological excavations, very little is known about the history of the period. However, we do know that as early as the Uruk and Jemdet Nasr Period (3500-3000 B.C.) some relationship existed between Egypt and Mesopotamia and whatever relationship there was, must have affected Phoenicia and Syria as trade relations between these two countries and Egypt started at a very early date. Some explain the relationship as a simultaneous Semitic penetration of the two countries, Mesopotamia and Egypt. However, after 3000 B.C. it seems that Egypt held Phoenicia as a subject state, or at least that the two countries were close allies with extensive trade relations. Be that as it may, we do know that Phoenicia, especially Byblos, supplied Egypt with the timber which she needed for her buildings, her boats, her furniture and fuel, and especially her funerary equipment. Vast quantities of cedar and pine timber were made into rafts and towed by boats from Byblos, mainly to Egypt, as early as 2800 B.C., during the reign of Khasekhem, the last king of the Second Dynasty or the first king of the Third. However, the relationship between the two countries may go back beyond that date into the Pre-Dynastic Period, and we may see in the legend of Set, Osiris, Isis and Horus a reflection of the struggle between the Semites and the Egyptians. Plutarch in recounting this legend says that Isis found the body of Osiris at Byblos enclosed within a tree which had in the meantime grown around it. In the struggle between Osiris and Set, [1] we see the contention between Upper and Lower Egypt; the Gerzeans were called the Sons of Horus. Set, under various names, continued to be one of the principal deities of the Delta, while his vanquished brother Osiris remained the god of the Egyptians. In the struggle between the Kingdom of Upper Egypt and the Kingdom of Lower Egypt we venture to suggest that there is a reflection of the struggle between the Amratians, who had infiltrated into the Delta and the Semitic Gerzeans who had entered Upper Egypt about 3400-3200 B.C., the period of Uruk in Mesopotamia. As in the later and similar expulsion of the Hyksos, the Egyptians followed, we venture to suggest, the foreigners into Syria and Phoenicia, making Byblos the focal point of their dominion abroad. The tenure of Byblos in some

---

[1] According to Egyptian mythology, Osiris, (possibly an allegorical representation of Egypt) although he was a benign god, was set upon by his brother Set and killed in order to gain Osiris's position as king of the gods, and his body was dismembered and cast away. Isis his sister-wife went in search of the body of Osiris and found it, as stated above, in a tree at Byblos.

18

sort of alliance was necessary, as Egypt, which was one of the largest timber-consuming countries of antiquity, lacked timber which was essential for its buildings, but especially for its funerary ritual. The solar barque of Ra' had to be made of cedar wood. Alabaster vases bearing the names of most of the kings of the III-VI Dynasties, but especially those of Pepi I and Pepi II of the Sixth Dynasty, were found in large quantities at Byblos during excavations, or by chance discovery. A large number of these vases are at the National Museum in Beirut and a smaller number may be seen at the Louvre Museum and the Archaeological Museum of the American University of Beirut. Furthermore the Palermo Stone states that 40 vessels loaded with *akh* wood arrived in Egypt during the reign of Senefru of the IV Dynasty. It is true that the cedar or pine forests were not in Phoenicia as previously explained, but in the uninhabited mountain range behind. One may ask why the Egyptian Pharoahs attempted to procure what timber they needed through Phoenician ports, and not overland. The reasons are not far to seek. First of all, transport by sea, in spite of its hazards, was cheaper and easier in those days than overland transport; secondly, in antiquity there were some forests close to the sea above Byblos and the other Phoenicians ports; thirdly, the overriding cause is indicated in the annals of Ancient Egypt: the Sinai Peninsula and Southern Palestine were infested at the time with predatory nomads, who made the overland trade routes between Egypt and Syria or Phoenicia unsafe. Several and repeated expeditions were undertaken against the nomads by the Pharoahs of the Vth and VIth Dynasties, but these were only partly successful on account of the elusiveness of the nomads, who would descend, seemingly from nowhere against caravans, rob them and disappear with lightning speed. [1] The Egyptian texts are full of imprecations against the depredations of these ancient Bedu robbers and their swift tactics of attack and escape.

During the anarchy which prevailed in Egypt under the VIIth-Xth Dynasties contact with Byblos whether by sea or by land seems to have been disrupted, and we may well suspect that the hold of Egypt over Phoenicia was broken; trade relations if

[1] Use was made of these tactics by Lawrence of Arabia in harassing Turkish columns during World War I.

3

they did not cease entirely ebbed considerably. Byblos lay in ruins at the time. [1]

At the end of the Sixth Dynasty, a wave of Semites, the Amurru or Amorites, taking advantage of the chaos prevailing in Egypt invaded Palestine, Syria and Phoenicia in the Twenty Third Century B.C. and later spread over into Mesopotamia. Their invasion was followed by wholesale destruction of cities and decimation of the original population. The south suffered considerably from their violence but the north seems to have escaped more of less unscathed. Byblos, Jericho and Beisan in Palestine were destroyed, but Ras Shamra survived the onslaught of the Amorites, only to fall victim to another attack from the north-east, the invasion of the Hurrians. [2] The history of the Near East during the Twenty-Third to Nineteenth Centuries B.C. is dark, but archaeology indicates that it was a period of general unrest. In Mesopotamia it witnessed the emergence of Assyria while the Guti [3] were disrupting the Empire of Naram Sin, and Ur was re-asserting Sumerian supremacy over the Semitic Akkadians for the last time. While the Amorites were ravaging Syria, Phoenicia and Palestine, the Hurrians started extending their power southward over North Syria.

Sometime during the Twenty-First Century B.C. a wave of metallurgists descended from Anatolia into the Western Horn of the Fertile Crescent and introduced their advanced lore in that industry. They were great adepts at their art, and from their arrival everywhere, whether at Ras Shamra or Byblos, we find them producing metal torques, toggle pins with an expanded head, and pierced near the top, biconical bronze beads, socketed lance-heads, and crescent-shaped socketed axe-heads. These folk came in the wake of the Amorite Invasion and before the arrival of the Pharoahs of the Twelfth Dynasty. Dr. Schaeffer calls them the

[1] M. Dunand in his excavations at Byblos found no remains of the period between the end of the VIth Dynasty (2290 B.C.) and the beginning of the XIIth (2000 B.C.).

[2] The Hurrians were an Armenoid folk who made their appearance in Asia Minor in the Second Millennium B.C.

[3] The Guti were barbarian tribesmen who overran Sumer and Akkad (Lower Mesopotamia) during the anarchy which set in after the death of the last king of the Dynasty of Akkad which was founded by Sargon I and ruled Babylonia for over a century, c.2200-2100 B.C.

torque wearers, and their arrival may well have had some relation
with that of the Hurrians.

By about 1950 B.C. the Pharoahs of the Twelfth Dynasty had
restored order and security in Egypt and re-asserted the prestige
of the country abroad. The inhabitants of Palestine, Phoenicia and
North Syria felt the impact of the strong pharoahs. Once again
Byblos, after an interval of nearly four hundred years became a
dependency of Egypt, and under its kings Ipshemuabi and Abishemu, close relations between the two countries were re-established,
Phoenicia exporting timber to Egypt and receiving in exchange
alabaster vases, pottery and furniture. It was during this period
that Sinuhe, a relative of King Senusert I, fled from Egypt after
having unsuccessfully attempted to raise a conspiracy against the
Pharoah. Sinuhe did not feel secure until he safely arrived in the
domain of the nomadic Bedu of the hinterland of Syria. It was
also during this period that Amenemhat IV (c.1850-1800 B.C.)
sent rich presents to his vassal Abishemu, the king of Byblos. In
the tomb of this King of Byblos, besides the objects actually sent
by the Pharoah which were manufactured in Egypt, other objects
which were manufactured in Phoenicia were discovered; the latter
objects include brooches, gold and silver vessels and other objects
which were strongly influenced by Egyptian art. The period was
an age of great prosperity for Southern Phoenicia judging by the
number of rich objects found in the tombs, in the temples and in
the royal palace. This prosperity was brought to an end sometime
between 1780 and 1730 B.C. when Egypt lapsed into her second
period of anarchy and dissolution. King Hammurabi of Babylon
captured North Syria and held it for thirty years. In 1750 a large
horde of Asianic tribes consisting amongst others of Hurrians,
threw themselves on North Syria, Phoenicia and Palestine, where
their numbers were swollen by the local Amorites and Canaanites,
the former subjects of Egypt; they invaded Egypt and held the
country in subjection for over 100 years. The Hyksos, as Manetho
calls the new comers, ruled Egypt tyrannically with an iron hand,
and aroused the deep hatred of the Egyptians for a long time to
come. Whether they actually conquered Upper and Lower Egypt,
or merely the Delta is not certain; but it is certain that they did
not hold Upper Egypt for long and eventually Upper Egypt
started a long and bitter life and death struggle with them. The

period of the Hyksos rule is called the Dark Ages of Alalakh by Woolley. In the absence of any documentary evidence we may well suspect that the 150 years of Hyksos rule in Phoenicia 1730-1580 was a period of darkness as well. However some cities of Phoenicia were occupied during the period, as a certain type of pottery which is generally associated with the Hyksos was discovered at Ras Shamra, Byblos and near Sidon. The Hyksos, coming from Asia, naturally showed favouritism to the Asiatic cities, but whether cities like Byblos which had such strong ties with Egypt benefited from this favouritism is not clear.

Eventually the Pharoahs of Upper Egypt succeeded in dislodging the Hyksos out of the Delta. Ahmes I, the founder of the XVIIIth Dynasty drove the Hyksos out of Egypt and followed them across the Sinai Desert as far as Sharuhen (probably Tell-Far'ah according to Albright). Thothmes I invaded Palestine, Phoenicia and Syria as far as the Euphrates. Phoenician cities sent tribute and submitted without a struggle. After this date, about 1525 B.C. we hear no more of the Hyksos who were either chased back to their Anatolian highlands, or absorbed by the Semitic element among them who settled in Phoenicia and Syria, the former homes of their ancestors, among the kinsmen whom their forefathers left behind a century or so earlier.

The expulsion of the Hyksos from Syria made it possible for the local cities to revert to pre-Hyksos days, when each city was completely independent of the other. The Prince of Kadesh-on-the-Orontes, [1] during the reign of Hatshepsut created a confederacy under his hegemony with a view to resisting a possible second invasion of Syria by Egypt. When in 1483 (or 1479) Hatshepsut died and Thothmes III her youthful son-in-law had shaken off his fetters, he immediately took the field against the Syrian confederacy headed by the Prince of Kadesh. At the famous historical battle ground of Megiddo, Thothmes defeated the confederacy, collected immense booty and took the wives of the Prince of Kadesh prisoners, but the Prince himself made his escape. It took Thothmes sixteen more campaigns finally to subdue the Prince of Kadesh and consolidate his gains; eventually Syria and Phoenicia became provinces of Egypt. Phoenicia gave Thothmes little trouble, no doubt on account of the historical association

[1] Probably Tell Nabi Mand, south of the Lake of Homs.

between the countries, but the hinterland revolted ceaselessly. In some of his campaigns, such as the sixth and the eighth, Thothmes came by sea using the Phoenician port of Simyra, near the Eleutheros, (Nahr el Kebir) as his base. Egypt possessing no navy at the time, Thothmes no doubt used Phoenician vessels for transporting his troops and supplies.

Phoenicia enjoyed a period of prosperity under the Pharoahs who succeeded Thothmes III, viz: Amenhotep II, Thothmes IV and the early part of the reign of Amenhotep III.

However, during the reign of the latter monarch it became soon apparent to his vassals and their neighbours that the Pharoah occupying the Egyptian throne was more interested in the pursuit of pleasure and luxurious living than in maintaining the security of the Empire. The Hittite king Shubiluliuma coveting Naharin, the fertile strip of land between the Euphrates and the Orontes, instigated the Amorite Prince of Coele-Syria, Abdashirta, to attack Phoenicia and so cut off Naharin from the south, so as to enable him to occupy it without fear of having to cross swords with the Egyptian army, whose renown at that time was as great as that of the hoplites of Sparta in later days, or of the *Grande Armée* of Napoleon in recent times. Abdashirta, who previously was a vassal of Egypt, revolted and proceeded to attack Phoenicia with the help of wild desert tribesmen called Habiru and Sa-Gaz. Shubiluliuma quietly walked into Naharin. It is significant that it was Ribadda the king of Byblos who first drew the attention of the Egyptian Pharoah to the insubordination of Abdashirta and begged him to send troops. The friends of Abdashirta at the Egyptian court did their utmost to throw dust in the eyes of Amenhotep III, but the flagrant and brazen hostility of Abdashirta finally induced the Pharoah to send troops and quell the revolt. Shubiluliuma quietly evacuated Naharin without waiting to be expelled by the Egyptian troops. Amenhotep III died in 1375 and was succeeded by his dilettante son Amenhotep IV or Akhenaten as he chose to call himself. [1] Shubiluliuma and Abdashirta

---

[1] Akhenaten proclaimed a new religion during the fourth year of his reign, declaring that Amen, Ra' and all the other Egyptian gods were mere fiction and that there is only one god who manifests himself to mankind through the sun-disk Aten, thereby causing a religious schism in Egypt to the neglect of the security and needs of his empire.

waited to see what type of Pharoah ascended the Egyptian throne. When they heard of the religious schism in Egypt and the pre-occupation of the Pharoah with his religious fads, Abdashirta again revolted and proceeded to attack Phoenicia; Shubiluliuma walked into Naharin. Abdashirta's son Aziru captured Simyra near the Eleutheros (Nahr el Kebir), and Arvad (Aradus) declared for Abdashirta. As no move was made by Akhenaten to dislodge Aziru from the Phoenician cities, Dushratta, the king of the Mitanni and an ally of Egypt, took matters into his own hands, moved into Phoenicia and recaptured Simyra. However, as still no help came from Egypt, and fearing an attack on his flank by Shubiluliuma, Dushratta retired.

Meanwhile, Ribadda of Byblos had been sending frantic appeals to Akhenaten for troops citing the fate of Simyra as an example, and fearing for his own safety. The revolt, however, spread, and Zimrida the King of Sidon was emboldened to join the rebels. His rival, Abimilki of Tyre, naturally joined Ribadda in imploring Egyptian aid. However, as Akhenaten was more interested in his religious fads rather than in acting as a school-master to what seemed to him a set of tiresome children, he turned a deaf ear to the entreaties of both Ribadda and Abimilki. As Ribadda anticipated, Aziru attacked Byblos, and Ribadda was obliged to escape to Berut whither he was followed by Aziru. Berut shared the fate of Byblos and fell into the hands of Aziru. Both Ribadda, and Ammunira the king of Berut, were put to death. [1] The entire coast of Phoenicia thus came under the rule of Aziru, the Amorite king of Lebanon and the hinterland.

The king of Ras Shamra-Ugarit became the vassal of the Hittites, while the rest of Phoenicia from Arvad to Tyre came under the hegemony of Aziru, who was himself a vassal of the Hittites.

Most of the letters exchanged between Ribadda, Abimilki, Dushratta, Amenhotep III and Akhenaten were discovered at Tell el Amarna, ancient Akhet Aten, the capital of Akhenaten. They were written in the Akkadian Semitic dialect in the cuneiform syllabic script. Thanks to these important documents our know-

---

[1] It is not clear whether Ribbada was put to death by Ammunira at the request of Aziru, or by Aziru himself.

ledge of the period is extremely rich. The letters not only give most valuable information, but they convey the stress and strain of the times and the anxiety of the various correspondents.

However, when Seti I, the second king of the XIXth Dynasty ascended the throne, he took the field against the Hittites and was able to recover Phoenicia and Palestine. His son and successor Rameses II carried on a long struggle with the Hittites for the recovery of the Empire of Thothmes, but after many a futile and fruitless campaign peace was eventually established and a treaty was signed between the two belligerents whereby Egypt retained Phoenicia and Palestine and Hatti maintained its suzerainty over the Amorites of the hinterland and Naharin. Shafatbaal and Ahiram were contemporary kings of Byblos and welcomed the return of the Egyptians to their country. Ahiram, a contemporary of Rameses II (1298-1232 B.C.) was buried in a stone sarcophagus carved with motifs strongly reminiscent of Egyptian art.

Egypt maintained its close relations with Phoenicia until the advent of the Aegeans. These people, having been driven from their homes in the Aegean by the Dorian invasions, threw themselves, in two waves, one on the Hittites in the north and the other on the Egyptians in the south. The north wave destroyed the Hittite Kingdom and descended into the north coast of Phoenicia, destroyed Alalakh and Ugarit forever and spread south probably as far as Byblos. The south wave was repelled by Rameses III at the Battle of Pelusium in 1149 B.C. but the Aegeans were allowed to settle in Palestine. They attacked most of the Phoenician cities, sacked Tyre and Sidon, and established their authority over the hinterland. Relations with Egypt were estranged. The Aegeans became masters of the Phoenician coast, and slowly they and the Canaanite inhabitants of Phoenicia assimilated to form a new race — Phoenicians — the race of mariners referred to by Homer. The Canaanites of Ugarit, Arvad, Simyra, Byblos, Berut, Sidon and Tyre prior to the Twelfth Century were never referred to as an ethnic group, but as Ugaritians, Arvadites, Simyrans, Gibelites, Berutians, Sidonians or Tyrians. From that time on, in addition to being called after their cities, they were referred to as Phoenicians, and it is proper that we should apply the term Phoenician only to the new race which resulted from the fusion of the proto-Phoenician Canaanites and the Aegeans. This race emerged in

the Twelfth Century B.C. on the Phoenician coast and established
a thalassocracy over the Mediterranean for over four centuries
and over the Aegean for at least three and a half centuries. They
were never eclipsed as a maritime nation until the rise of Venice,
Genoa and Pisa in the Middle Ages. It is this fusion of races which
heralded the Golden Age of Phoenician greatness.

The Golden Age of Phoenicia

From about 1150 B.C. to 853 B.C. the various Phoenician
cities were independent, perhaps for the first time in their history.
They, especially Tyre and Sidon, sent their galleys far and wide
in quest of trade, and established factories or trading stations in
Greece and North Africa in places such as Thebes, Corinth and
Utica. Carthage was founded about 814 B.C., but it was not only
a trading station, but a city, the new city, as its name indicates.
Although Tyre and Sidon replaced Byblos as the chief port of
Phoenicia, Byblos kept pace with the two new metropoleis and it
was from Byblos that the alphabet found its way into Greece. A
peace-loving nation avoiding war and conflict, unless peace clashed
with their independence or their commercial interests, the Phoenicians sought to gain their ends by diplomacy and amicable relations. Hiram of Tyre made a treaty with Solomon of Israel. Ahab
further cemented the friendly relations between the two countries
by marrying Jezebel the daughter of Ithobaal, king of Sidon.

However, the kings of Byblos refused to continue as vassals
of Egypt. When Herihor (c.1085 B.C.) the founder of the Twenty-
First Dynasty in Egypt, despatched Wenamen to Byblos to procure
cedar wood for the barge of Amen, Zakarbaal the king of Byblos
would not receive him and gave him orders to quit the city,
although Wenamen explained that he was prepared to pay for
the wood in silver, albeit a paltry sum that would not satisfy the
the cupidity of the Phoenician trader-king. Later, however, when
Wenamen received more silver and other presents through a
messenger, the desired wood was delivered.

The names of the kings of the various cities we know either
from the monuments, from Herodotus, Menander or from the
Bible. Besides Zakarbaal the names of his successors Abibaal,
Elibaal and Yahumelek of Byblos have come down to us. But we
are better acquainted with the kings of Tyre from traditions.

Hiram I, the contemporary of Solomon, the king of Israel,

after a long and prosperous reign was succeeded by Baal-Tsur of whom we do not know much beyond his name. His successor Abd-Ashtart was deposed by a court conspiracy. After a short period of anarchy, Ithobaal, the high priest of Ashtart, who belonged to the legitimate royal family, regained the throne. It was this Ithobaal who gave his daughter Jezebel in marriage to Ahab the king of Israel. Jezebel was a devout worshipper of Ashtart and in her new role as queen of Israel she brought with her the worship of Baal and Ashtart and sought to impose it on Israel and perhaps supplant the worship of Jahweh. Her daughter Athaliah, no doubt under the tutelage of her mother, sought to impose the Phoenician cults in Judah, having been married to Jehoram the king of Judah.

Hitherto we have been on sure ground as most of the events described by Herodotus and others are corroborated in the Bible. For the following fifty years or so, we face a dilemma; the events narrated are linked with the foundation of Carthage and some fanciful legends have been interwoven with the historical narrative attributing the causes of the foundation to flimsy affairs, and setting aside the real historical reasons which brought about the foundation of the city. A grandson of Ithobaal, Mathan, succeeded to the throne about 850 BC. He left a daughter, Elissa (Dido), and a son called Pygmalion. Menander states that Elissa married her uncle Zakarbaal (Acherbas) the high priest of Melqart and succeeded her father, a very unusual state of affairs in the ancient world. Pygmalion assassinated Acherbas and deposed his sister Elissa. Elissa with her partisans fled to Cyprus, and from thence to North Africa where she founded a New City, Carthage. This is a tradition which we cannot accept as authentic history. Let us examine the historical facts and search for the real causes which led to the foundation of the most important Phoenician city overseas and see how much they tally with this tale.

Ever since the Tell el-Amarna Period, Assyria, in North Mesopotamia, had been gaining in strength and importance. Ashur-Uballit the king of Assyria, a contemporary of Shubiluliuma (1375-1340 B.C.), the king of Hatti [1] was strong enough to attack

[1] The Hittites were a race of Indo-European tribes who made their appearance in Central Asia Minor at the beginning of the Second Millennium B.C. In process of time they spread into the hill country situated in the bend

the Mitanni. Shubiluliuma, however, drove him out, and made himself arbiter in the succession dispute among Dushratta's sons.

Ashur-Uballit was succeeded by a line of unambitious kings until Shalmaneser I, (1295-1250 B.C.) who extended the territory of Assyria over Mitanni and Babylon. The next king, Tukulti-Enurta (1250-1241 BC.), fastened the yoke of Assyria even more securely. A long period then followed in which there was a tug of war struggle between Babylon and Ashur for political supremacy over Mesopotamia. Both states contended for dominion over each other with varying fortunes until the accession of Tiglath Pileser I who ascended the throne of Assyria about 1110 B.C. Tiglath Pileser extended his dominion over Babylon in the south-east and advanced as far as the Mediterranean on the West, capturing Arvad as well as other Phoenician cities on the north coast of Phoenicia. After him Assyria lapsed into lethargy for over two hundred years. With the accession of Ashur-nasirpal II in 883, Assyria entered on a career of aggressive conquest. Ashur-nasirpal, in addition to other conquests, occupied Naharin, and crossed the Orontes into Phoenicia. He exacted tribute from Tyre, Sidon, Byblos and Arvad. His successor Shalmaneser III (859-824 B.C.) heralded his accession with an unprovoked attack on Naharin in anticipation of a revolt. This wanton action was followed by an attack on the Aramaean king of Damascus, Ben-Hadad II. Both kings claimed victory at the Battle of Qarqar in 853 B.C., but as no territorial changes ensued, the battle was probably indecisive. Assyrian rule, however, being anything but benign, led a large contingent of Tyrians and Sidonians to leave their homeland and found a new city (Kart Hadashah) at Carthage in North Africa soon after the battle. Around this event tradition wove the fanciful tale of Elissa and Pygmalion. Are we right in assuming that Pygmalion or whatever his true Phoenician name was, who may have been pro-Assyrian, deposed and murdered Acherbas (Zakar-Baal) the leader of the anti-Assyrian party? The Assyrians, however, prevailed, and the

of the river Halys (modern Kizil Irmak) subdued the inhabitants of the area who were called Hattians and adopted their name. From the seventeenth to the fourteenth century B.C. their history is a series of rises and falls until the accession of Shubiluliuma. This king, who was a contemporary of Amenhotep III and Akhenaten, profited by the attacks of the Amorites, Habiru and Sa-Gaz on the Egyptian Empire, by seizing North Syria and Phoenicia.

party of Elissa had to leave and seek their fortune elsewhere in the wide dominions of the Phoenicians.

Relations with Assyria, Neo-Babylonia and Persia./

From about 850 B.C. onwards, we find the Tyrians, Gibelites and Arvadites paying tribute to Assyria. Tiglath Pileser III, (745-727) lists the names of the kings of Tyre and Sidon (Hiram II), Gebal and Arvad among his tributaries. In 725 there was a general revolt against Assyria led by Hosea of Israel and Luli I King of Tyre and Sidon; it was instigated by that "broken reed" Egypt. Shalmaneser V (727-722 B.C.) the king of Assyria took the field against the rebels and laid siege to Samaria in 724 B.C. Samaria was captured by his son Sargon II (722-705 B.C.) in 722 B.C., but Tyre held out for twenty one more years. In 701 B.C. Sennacherib, Sargon's successor, defeated the confederates and Luli sought refuge by flight to Cyprus. Ithobaal was made king of Tyre in his place. Sennacherib recorded the event on a stele at Nahr el-Kalb. Sennacherib in this stele mentions the names of the kings of Byblos and Arvad, but not of Sidon which was at the time under the tutelage of Tyre. Abdmilkut, king of Sidon revolted against Esarhaddon, the king of Assyria, in 678 B.C. The revolt was put down with great severity. Abdmilkut, following the example of Luli, sought refuge in flight by sea, but he was apprehended "and caught like a fish from the sea" and decapitated. Sidon was utterly destroyed, and its inhabitants were put to the sword. New inhabitants were transplanted from the Persian Gulf to the Phoenician coast by Esarhaddon in order to found a new city in place of the Old Sidon. Baal, the king of Tyre, was made a vassal king, and a treaty was signed to give legal recognition to this fact. In spite of this treaty, when Tirhaqa, the king of Egypt, instigated Tyre to revolt, he found a willing ear. Esarhaddon quelled the revolt without difficulty and Luli II of Tyre and Sidon was captured. During the reign of Ashurbanipal, Tyre revolted for the third time. The Assyrian king was unable to capture the island fortress, but contented himself with raiding continental Tyre (Palaeatyros) and taking Yahumelek, the crown prince, with him as hostage. Arvad, in spite of its insular isolation, paid tribute. The king, Yakin-lou, accompanied by his children, personally brought the tribute to Niniveh and laid it before the Assyrian monarch.

After the destruction of Niniveh and the Assyrian Empire by

the combined forces of Babylon and Media in 612 B.C. the various
Phoenician cities regained their independence, and immediately
established relations with Egypt, welcoming its Saïte King, Necho II,
when he advanced into Palestine, Phoenicia and Syria. However
at the Battle of Carchemish in 605 B.C. Necho II was defeated
and fled to Egypt followed by the victor Nebuchadrezzar, the
crown prince of Neo-Babylonia. Phoenicia, Syria and Palestine
had to accept the Babylonian yoke. Apries, (Hophra of the Bible)
the king of Egypt, was not happy at the turn events had taken, so
taking a page out of Tirhaqa's book, he instigated Tyre, Sidon and
Judaea to revolt. Nebuchadrezzar, after chasing Apries out of
Phoenicia, descended on Jerusalem and destroyed the city, taking
part of the population into captivity. Then, having secured his
flank, he turned his attention to Tyre, which he had to besiege
for thirteen years before being able finally to capture it. He
dethroned Ithobaal II, the king of Tyre, and put Baal II, a sub-
servient king, in his place. Baal reigned for a period of ten years
after which Tyre followed Carthage by adopting a republican
form of government under the leadership of a shofet or magistrate.
Phoenicia remained in a state of vassalage to Babylonia until
Cyrus, the king of Persia, captured Babylon in 538 B.C., whereupon
Phoenicia changed masters again. Sidon now became the leading
city of Phoenicia, superseding Tyre which started on its decline.
To make matters worse for her, Carthage severed all political
connection with its mother-city. Darius I, the king of Persia,
divided his Empire into twenty satrapies or provinces, with
Phoenicia, Cyprus and Syria forming the fifth. The Phoenicians
at the outset collaborated with their new masters, and the Phoenician navy took a leading part in the wars of Darius and Xerxes
against Greece. The king of Sidon was also appointed the Admiral
of the Persian Navy. However, Persian rule during the fourth
century B.C. was not as benign as in the early fifth. The Achae-
maenid throne was occupied by a line of cruel, harim ridden despots.
This situation gave rein to the various satraps to indulge in inter-
necine wars amongst each other and to disrupt the Persian Empire.
When Evagoras, the Greek tyrant of Cyprus descended on the
Phoenician coast in 392 B.C., he found a ready welcome at Tyre
which had been suffering from the exactions of the Persian satraps.
Straton I, the king of Sidon, showed distinct leanings towards the

Greeks and when some satraps rebelled in 362 B.C. he joined them. In 346 B.C. Tabnit, king of Sidon rebelled against the Persians. Artaxerxes III came up with a large army. Tabnit, although feigning patriotism, offered to deliver the city to the Persian king. When the Sidonians heard of this, they shut themselves up in their houses and set fire to the city, perishing in the flames. Every male, female, child and beast was exterminated; all the manuscripts, archives, books, treasures and works of art in the city perished. A new city was soon built, but Sidon lost its foremost place among the cities of Phoenicia. We hear of names of such kings as Strato II, Tabnit, Eshmunazar and Bodashtart, but we do not know much about them beyond the fact that the sarcophagi in which Tabnit and Eshmunazar were buried have come to light; the former is now in the Constantinople Museum, while the latter is in the Louvre. It is possible also, that the famous Alexander sarcophagus, which was discovered at Sidon, was made for Bodashtart. Bodashtart is also noted for a temple of Eshmun (Adonis) which he restored at Sidon.

Relations with Greeks

The Phoenicians and Greeks appear as implacable enemies throughout the historical period. Herodotus cites the rape of Io [1] as the principal cause for this hatred. To this we venture to add the fact that the Phoenicians, or at least a large part of them, never forgot the tradition that the Greeks expelled their ancestors from their homes, and dwelt in their land. Another cause of hatred and envy was of course the commercial rivalry of the two nations.

To the Greeks, all non-Greeks, especially the Asiatics, were strangers whom they styled as barbarians. However, the word did not signify the ugly connotation that it acquired later as a synonym of savagery and lack of civilization. In fact some Greeks admired the achievement of the Babylonians in astronomy and science, and did not disdain learning and adopting Babylonian and Egyptian lore through the Phoenicians whether in science or in commerce, and put it to their own use, albeit they despised the political servility of the Asiatics, which they could not comprehend.

[1] Io is alleged to have been a Greek princess who was abducted by a Phoenician captain while she was examining wares on the sea-shore which were brought by a Phoenician vessel. The Greeks accused the Phoenicians of abducting her by force, and the Phoenicians alleged that she was willing as she was enamoured of the captain.

The first clash between Greeks and Phoenicians probably occurred in Cyprus. From the eleventh or even the twelfth century B.C. Cyprus and Phoenicia were so closely linked that it can be stated that the culture of the two countries was identical. Furthermore, ethnologically the Cypriotes were descended from the Aegeans, who, as we have seen were in a large measure the co-progenitors of the Phoenicians. During the eighth to sixth century B.C., the great period of Greek colonization, some Greek colonies were established in Cyprus but not very many. When, however, Sargon II invaded Cyprus about 711 B.C. he found one Phoenician and nine Greek kings in the island. What is meant by "Greek" is not very clear. That some Hellenes were in the island is beyond doubt, but the Achaeans also spoke a Greek dialect as we now know from the decipherment of the Linear B script, and some of the "Greek kings" or tyrants in the island may have been Aegean rather than Hellenic Greek.

The Phoenician navy transported the troops of Darius I in 490 B.C. from Samos to Naxos, Carystus and Eritrea most willingly, as the subjugation of Greece would have meant that the Aegean world would be re-opened to Phoenician trade. Defeated at Marathon, the Persians returned for a second round under Xerxes in 480 B.C., only to be utterly defeated in the naval battle of Salamis where the bulk of the Perso-Phoenician navy was destroyed and the remainder was annihilated at Mycale near Samos in 479. A third clash took place at the Eurymedon in Asia Minor in 468 B.C. where two hundred Phoenician vessels were sunk. After the destruction of the Athenian Empire in 404 B.C., the Persian Court carried on a game of intrigue in Greece which fostered disunity and led to incessant wars between the various Greek city-states so as to prevent them combining into a united force which might have spelt danger to the Persian Empire.

When Greek unity was eventually achieved by force by Philip of Macedon, one of the foremost plans that Philip formulated was an invasion of Asia in order to put a stop to the machinations of the Persian court. Philip did not live to accomplish this task, but left it to his son, Alexander the Great. Alexander, at one fell blow delivered at the Granicus, secured Asia Minor in 334 B.C. to Greek civilization. Another blow delivered at Issus in 333 B.C. laid the way open for him to Phoenicia. Possessing no fleet of adequate strength and not wishing to leave his rear open to the onslaughts of the Phoenician navy, Alexander instead of pursuing Darius to Babylon and Susa marched across Phoenicia capturing the Phoenician ports of Arvad, Byblos and Sidon, without meeting resistance. He made arrangements for the restoration of Sidon which was still suffering from the effects of the fire of 346 B.C., and advanced southwards.

Outside Tyre he was met by a deputation of Tyrians who informed him that they would not block his passage, but they also indicated that in his struggle with the Persian King, they wished to remain strictly neutral and that they would neither permit him or the Persian king, Darius III Condomannus, to enter their city. Alexander said that he would respect the neutrality of Tyre but he asked to be allowed to sacrifice to his patron deity, Melqart-Herakles, in the temple in their city. The Tyrians refused considering this action a breach of neutrality; whereupon Alexander decided to take the city by force, as he did not wish to leave such a strong island fortress in his rear. As stated previously there were two Tyres, continental Tyre or Palaeatyros and the island fortress. Alexander subdued Palaeatyros without difficulty and destroyed it; he then proceeded to build a causeway from the mainland to the island with the debris of the destroyed city. The Tyrians retaliated by shooting his labourers. Alexander built two movable wooden towers at either end of the causeway and set up a leather curtain between them in order to shield his labourers. The Tyrians sent ships full of inflammables which set fire to the curtain and towers. Alexander was baffled and proceeded to widen the causeway. Meanwhile the galleys of Aradus, Byblos and Sidon who had been harassing the Aegean in Alexander's rear, on learning of the submission of their cities, returned to their home ports, and were immediately put to the task of besieging Tyre by sea. Great headway was made with the causeway, and the siege engines were brought up against the city walls. The Tyrians threw big rocks outside their walls in order to prevent the siege engines reaching them, but these were towed away by the Phoenician ships. Eventually a breach was made in the south wall of the city. The city was taken by assault in August 332 B.C. after a siege of nine months. 8000 persons perished in the street fighting and 30,000 were taken prisoner and sold into slavery. Never had Tyre experienced such a determined siege, or put up such a stout resistance in the long range of its chequered history. Even the siege of Tyre by Nebuchadrezzar which lasted thirteen years (587-574) did not equal the ferocity of the struggle for the independence of the city, and the equal determination of Alexander to subdue it. In no other siege in history was such ingenuity shown in the methods of attack, or in the counter-measures of defence which developed during the course of the siege of Tyre in 333-332 B.C.

During the short reign of Alexander the Phoenician cities enjoyed a certain measure of autonomy. However, the impact of Hellenism began to manifest itself in the art and architecture of the time as we shall see when we come to discuss Phoenician art.

During the struggle between the Diadochi, Alexander's companions, Phoenicia often witnessed the march of Macedonian soldiers across its territory and the mountains of Lebanon must have often re-echoed the tramp of soldiers' feet as the phalanxes of Ptolemy moved to Egypt soon after Alexander's death, followed by those of Perdiccas. The phalanxes of Antigonus moved north and south several times between the Council of Tri-Paradisos in 321 B.C. and the Battle of Ipsos in 301 B.C., for Antigonus made several attempts to unify Alexander's Empire and retain it for his own family. He undertook many campaigns against Egypt with that end in view. However, as a result of the Battle of Ipsos in 301 B.C., Phoenicia was occupied by Ptolemy and attached to Egypt. A long struggle ensued between the Seleucids and the Ptolemies for Phoenicia and Coelo-Syria, but the Ptolemies of Egypt retained their hold on Coele-Syria until the Battle of Paneion in 200 B.C. when Antiochus III defeated Ptolemy V Epiphanes, and captured Phoenicia. Phoenicia remained under Seleucid domination until the disruption of the Seleucid Kingdom after the death of Antiochus IV Epiphanes, when some Phoenician cities such as Aradus [1] and Marathus regained their autonomy, to be followed later by other cities in the south. Byblos and Tripoli were ruled by tyrants. By about 112 B.C. practically all Phoenician cities became independent, and indulged in rivalry and sometimes open warfare with one another. As an example of the latter, mention may be made of the destruction of Marathus at the hands of the Arvadites in 146 B.C.

[1] Aradus actually started minting its own coins as early as 259 B.C.

34

The Phoenician cities remained independent until 64 B.C. when Pompey visited Syria, Phoenicia and Palestine, put an end to the Seleucid Dynasty and reconstituted Syria and Phoenicia as a Roman Province. The Phoenician cities continued to enjoy their previous autonomy and to mint their own coins, but they became client-allies of Rome, and the governor of Syria, with the rank first of pro-praetor and later of pro-consul, held supervisory control over the affairs of the various cities in both Phoenicia and Syria. Berytus, which had been destroyed in 143 B.C. by Diodotus, an usurper who assumed the name of Tryphon, was refounded by Augustus in 14 B.C.

Under the Romans, profiting from the *Pax Romana*, the Phoenician cities became great centres of industry, trade, progress and wealth. Blown glass was invented at Sidon which brought untold wealth to the country. Trade between east and west passed through the Phoenician cities and was carried in Phoenician merchantmen. This wealth is reflected in the cultural progress of the country. A school of philosophy was established at Sidon on the pattern of the Peripatetic School of Aristotle. At Tyre a rival Stoic school of philosophy was maintained. Byblos was a great city of learning. It produced the great Philo of Byblos and Hermippus the grammarian. Thus the Phoenician cities were not only centres of trade and industry but became centres of learning as well. Septimius Severus established a law school in Beirut, which had a high repute. Among its teachers were the famous lawyers Papinian and Ulpian who later held high offices in the Roman Empire.

Christianity gained a strong foothold in Phoenicia at an early age. St. Paul found a church already in existence at Tyre on his return from Greece about A.D. 58. The Emperors Valerian, Diocletian and Maximinus Daia were perturbed by the large number of Christians in the country in the third century A.D. that they singled them out for especially heavy persecution. In the fourth century A.D. Tyre was one of the strongholds of Arianism; several church Councils met there to condemn Athanasius of Alexandria and his doctrines.

Under the Byzantine Emperors, Phoenicia held a very important place. Since it was one of the richest provinces of the Empire, the tribute received from it enriched the imperial fiscus. It was selected for special treatment, for it lay athwart the land and sea routes, between Constantinople and Jerusalem. A law school of such great repute had been established at Beirut in days gone by during the reign of Septimius Severus that, when Justinian wanted to codify the laws of the Empire he sought the aid of Dorotheos, the head of the Beirut law school to help in the task. It was during Justinian's reign that some monks introduced the silkworm from China to Phoenicia and Syria, and thus started an industry which brought great fame to the two countries concerned, and became one of their leading industries.

It was through Syria and Phoenicia that Chosroes II invaded Palestine and carried away the True Cross in AD. 614.

Byzantine rule in Phoenicia was very beneficial. The country enjoyed three centuries of peace and prosperity reflected in the great historical works and patristic literature of the time and the numerous ruins which were teaming with life and activity at the time. No one in A.D. 628 could have foretold that within six or eight years all this area would soon be submerged by a warlike race which had hitherto been relegated to the obscurity of its desert home on account of the lack of a leader. When the leader, Muhammad, was found, the new virile nation of the Arabs swept everything before it including one great empire, the Sassanian Empire of Persia, and the larger part of a second, the Byzantine Empire of Constantinople. The history of this new nation has been adequately treated by Professor Hitti and others and it is a convenient point to stop here, referring the reader to the great work of Professor Hitti, the *History of the Arabs* for the subsequent history of Syria, Phoenicia, Palestine, Iraq and Egypt.

Phoenicians Overseas

No study of the Phoenician nation would be complete if it did not include a discussion of the colonies and offshoots of Phoenicia abroad. Reference has already been made to the factories and trading stations which were established by the Phoenicians in various places on the shores of the Mediterranean including its offshoot the Aegean. Phoenician foundations in Greece such as Thebes and Corinth were soon absorbed by the Boeotians and Dorians. The foundations in Cyprus however persisted well into the Persian Period. The foundations at Kition, Narnaca (modern Larnaca) and elsewhere soon developed into large cities. We have seen how Elissa and Luli, when fleeing from the Assyrians sought refuge in Cyprus, because Cyprus at the time was just as truely Phoenician as Tyre or Sidon, and the fugitives could count on a ready welcome and asylum among their relatives. When Esarhaddon in 672 invaded Cyprus he found one Phoenician, as well as nine other Greek kings ruling different parts of the island. Earlier the Phoenicians formed an even larger proportion.

But for the greatest expansion of the Phoenicians we have to go further afield to the western basin of the Mediterranean. We have seen how Carthage was founded soon after 814 B.C. by fugitives from Tyre and Sidon, at the beginning of the Assyrian expansion. A second wave of emigrants left Tyre during the reign of Nebuchadrezzar, during or soon after the great siege, in the sixth century B.C. From now on Carthage assumed a great role in the Western Mediterranean championing the cause of Semitism against that of the Indo-European Greeks of Sicily.

Carthage established trading centres in Sicily, Corsica and Sardinia. When some Greeks from Rhodes and the neighbouring city of Cnidus attempted to found a settlement at the extreme western point of Sicily, the Carthaginians attacked them and destroyed the settlement in 580 B.C. Carthage had set her eyes on Sicily at an early date and an expedition under Malchus attempted to wrest the island from the Greeks in 560 B.C. But Phalaris, the Greek tyrant of Acragas, opposed them effectively.

In 545 B.C., when Cyrus captured Sardis and destroyed the kingdom of Lydia and inherited its suzerainty over Ionia, some Phocaeans left their city in Ionia and founded a colony at Alalia in Corsica, in preference to a state of vassalage under Cyrus. The Carthaginians destroyed Alalia in 535 B.C. Trading stations were established by the Carthaginians at Gozo Malta and the south coast of Spain. From then on Carthage exercised her hegemony over the Western Mediterranean, incessantly clashing with the Greeks because of the clash of commercial interests.

In 482 B.C., on the eve of the invasion of Greece by Xerxes, his loyal Phoenician subjects induced their brethren the Carthaginians to attack Gelon, the tyrant of Syracuse, so as to prevent that powerful potentate from sending aid to the mother country. The Greek Dorians and Ionians in Sicily were at loggerheads with one another at the time and gave Carthage the necessary excuse for sending an expedition against Gelon. Theron, the tyrant of Acragas, drove Terillus, the tyrant of Himera, out of his city. Terillus appealed to Carthage, and Theron appealed to his son-in-law Gelon of Syracuse.

Carthage sent an expedition under Hamilcar. Hamilcar landed at Panormus (modern Palermo, a Carthaginian station) and besieged Himera. As was usual in those days before joining in battle, the Carthaginian general decided to sacrifice to Baal Yam (Poseidon) the god of the sea. He wrote to the friendly Greek city of Selinus to ask for horsemen to direct him in the ritual of sacrifice. His letter fell into the hands of Gelon, who sent some of his own horsemen with orders to fall on the Carthaginians as soon as they were admitted into their camp. The Carthaginians admitted Gelon's horsemen who immediately killed Hamilcar by the altar of Poseidon and set fire to his ships. In the ensuing battle the Carthaginians were utterly routed and sued for peace, which was granted on the most humiliating terms.

After the Battle of Himera, the Carthaginians were restricted to a small enclave at the extreme west end of the island comprising about one fifth of the island in size.

Hostilities were resumed about seventy years later by the covetous action of the Greek city of Selinus. Selinus had been in the habit of encroaching on the lands of her neighbour Segesta. The first demand came in 416. Segesta appealed to Athens who unwisely sent the ill-fated Sicilian expedition. [1]

In 409 Selinus made another demand. Segesta appealed to Carthage and the latter sent an expedition under Hannibal, grandson of the Hamilcar who perished at Himera. Hannibal landed at Lilybaeum at the extreme west end of the island and marched against Selinus. After a short siege, a breach was made in the walls of Selinus and the city was captured and sacked. The aim of the expedition was thus accomplished. But Hannibal remembered the trick played by Gelon on his grandfather Hamilcar and felt it was his filial duty to avenge his grandfather's death. He marched against Himera and besieged it. Deiocles, the *strategos* of Syracuse, came to its relief with a force of five thousand men. By that time Hannibal had made a breach in the walls, and in order to wreak his vengeance on the city he allowed a report to spread that he was marching against Syracuse. Deiocles was

[1] See Bury: *History of Greece*, pp. 466-484.

deceived and marched home to protect his city. Hannibal then took Himera by assault, sacked the city and razed it to the ground. Three thousand citizens of Himera were sacrificed on the very spot where Hamilcar was supposed to have fallen. A new city was founded by the Carthaginians on the site of Himera which was renamed Thermae, in order to obliterate the former name forever.

In 406 B.C. Hannibal wanted to resume the offensive against the Greeks because of the ill-considered action of a Greek private army. He offered immunity from attack to Acragas, if that city would keep neutral. The citizens of Acragas refused and proceeded to put their defences in order under the supervision of a Spartan mercenary captain called Dexippus. Hannibal then began the siege of Acragas, establishing two camps, one east and one west of Acragas. The Carthaginians then had a series of reverses. First of all a plague broke out in one of their camps, removing Hannibal who was succeeded by his brother Himilco. Secondly, a large force of Greeks, collected from Syracuse and elsewhere, attacked one of the Carthaginian camps and captured it. But the Acragantians failed to sally forth and help the relieving force, thus losing a golden opportunity. Furthermore Himilco, whose supplies were running short, intercepted supplies destined for Acragas. The tables were reversed and Acragas was put to dire straits. Their Greek allies, disgusted with the citizens of Acragas, deserted them. The Acragantians in their turn, left their city at night. The following day it was occupied by the Carthaginians. This battle had great repercussions in Greek Sicily, which brought about the tyranny of Dionysios who was to rule all Sicily for the space of nearly forty years.

After the capture of Acragas the Carthaginians moved east against Gela. Dionysios the tyrant of Syracuse removed the inhabitants of Gela and the neighbouring city of Camarina to Syracuse. The Carthaginians then occupied the two cities. A treaty was negotiated with Carthage on the principle of *uti possidetis* thus confirming the Carthaginian occupation of Acragas, Gela, Camarina, Selinus and Thermae and all the territory between them, approximately three quarters of the island. In return for this Carthage recognized the suzerainty of Dionysios over the rest of Greek Sicily which did not all belong to him yet.

During the next six years 404-398 B.C. Dionysios was busy consolidating his position and strengthening his army. In 398 B.C.

he was ready to launch an offensive against Carthage. Without much difficulty he recaptured Gela, Camarina and Acragas. Thermae declared for him. Only Segesta refused to join him. At the head of an army of 80,000 mostly Campanian mercenaries, Dionysios advanced against the island fort of Motya off Lilybaeum. He proceeded to build a causeway from the mainland to the island, and when that was finished, he threw up siege towers against the city. The Motyans did not demonstrate the ingenuity of the Tyrians sixty six years later. Himilco came with a large fleet for the relief of Motya but was driven off by the deadly catapults recently invented by Dionysios. Motya was taken in a night attack amid the most horrible carnage in history, which only a tyrant could put into operation. All prisoners were sold into slavery. Carthage bestirred itself and sent Himilco with a large force. On his arrival Dionysios retired to Syracuse. Himilco recaptured Motya and founded Lilybaeum on the shore opposite Motya in the bay of the same name. Himilco then advanced west unopposed, captured Messana and razed it to the ground. In a naval battle off Catane, the Greek fleet was heavily defeated and Syracuse was besieged. At this stage an unlooked for ally of the Greeks manifested itself in the form of a plague which decimated the Carthaginian camp. The Carthaginian fleet was attacked and defeated in the Great Harbour of Syracuse, and Dionysios attacked the Carthaginian camp on land, defeating them with great slaughter, but at the same time to impress on the Syracusans the necessity of keeping him in power, he allowed the Carthaginians to escape.

After this, war continued sporadically between Dionysios and Carthage with varying success until his death in 367 B.C.

During the following twenty years the Greeks in Sicily were too busy fighting each other to pay much attention to Carthage until the Greeks themselves dragged the Carthaginians in. Some Greeks, being tired of the ceaseless wars in Sicily, sent to Corinth the mother city of all Dorian colonies in Sicily, to send someone to regulate the affairs of the Greeks in the island. Corinth sent Timoleon. However, Hiketas, the tyrant of Leontini opposed Timoleon, and implored Carthaginian aid. Carthage sent a force under Mago's command, who entered the Great Harbour at Syracuse and captured the city. At this juncture Timoleon arrived. The Greek soldiers of Timoleon and Hiketas started talking.

Mago noticed this, immediately suspected treachery and sailed off. Timoleon then proceeded to recapture and organize the Greek cities one after the other. Fearing aggression on her section of the island, Carthage sent a force under Hamilcar and Hasdrubal to Lilybaeum. This force marched on Syracuse but was met at the Crimisus River by Timoleon, who routed it completely, aided by a heavy storm which blew in the faces of the Carthaginians, many of whom were drowned in the river, after it had swollen by the torrential rain. Peace was established with Carthage and the Halycus was fixed as the boundary between the Greeks and Carthaginians. This boundary line remained static until the time of Agathocles, tyrant (319 B.C.) and later King (306 B.C.) of Syracuse who took up the cudgels for Hellenism against Carthage and well-nigh brought her to her knees, had it not been for the rival Greek cities who compelled him to come to an understanding with Carthage. He was about to renew the struggle in the fateful year 289 B.C. when he was overtaken by death.

After the death of King Agathocles, the Greeks in Sicily were hard pressed by the Carthaginians. Together with Taras, (Tarentum) which was under pressure by Rome, Syracuse sent an appeal to Greece for aid. Pyrrhus, the king of Epirus, in whom most of the Hellenistic kings saw a dangerous rival, was provided by them with money, men and elephants and sent to relieve the Greeks of Magna Graecia. Carthage and Rome combined to get rid of him and after his departure Rome was ready to enter into conflict with Carthage over Sicily and thus start the Punic Wars which were to bring about the destruction of Carthage. The Western Mediterranean basin was too narrow for two such great powers as that of Rome and Carthage, and both sides awaited a *casus belli* to start hostilities.

The Punic Wars

Before we enter into a lengthy discussion of the Punic Wars it would be highly desirable to examine briefly the relations between Carthage and Rome anterior to the conflict.

We first hear of the relations between the two cities in 348 B.C. when a treaty of friendship was concluded between the two cities, which was renewed in 306 B.C. In 279 B.C. a military alliance was concluded between the two cities against Pyrrhus, the king of Epirus. In spite of these treaties Rome was suspicious of Carthage.

The First Punic War

What brought about the clash was a small incident at Messana. In 289 B.C. Messana, a Greek city in Sicily on the strait of the same name was seized by Campanian mercenaries who had previously been engaged by Agathocles, and who called themselves Mamertines or the sons of Mars. In 264 B.C. Hiero, the tyrant of Syracuse, proceeded to attack them and besieged Messana. The Mamertines appealed for help to a Carthaginian fleet which was cruising in the area. The Carthaginian admiral forced Hiero to raise the siege. Instead of leaving, however, he stayed on and the Mamertines found that they had gotten rid of the devil only to fall into the deep sea. They were thus compelled to appeal to Rome. Rome decided to send a relief force which secured Messana without bloodshed. Carthage however sent an expedition to recover Messana and Rome sent reinforcements to hold it. Both sides drifted into hostilities without actually declaring war.

The Carthaginians and Syracusans formed a military alliance against Rome and besieged Messana. Appius Claudius arrived from Rome and drove a wedge between the two allies. Meanwhile another Roman army under Manlius Valerius besieged Syracuse. Although the siege was not successful, Hiero was detached from his alliance with Carthage.

Carthage sent an army of 50,000 men based on Acragas, which from now on must be called by its Latin name Agrigentum (modern Gergente). The Romans advanced on Agrigentum, stormed the city and sacked it (262 B.C.).

At this stage, the war reached a stalemate as the Romans realized that in order to defeat Carthage they must meet her on her own ground, the sea. So Rome resolved to build her first fleet. In 260 B.C. the Roman fleet was ready and put to sea. The first naval engagement took place at Mylae, where the Romans gained their first naval victory, sinking and capturing about fifty Punic vessels.

In 256 B.C. the Romans felt strong enough to venture an invasion of Africa. The consuls Atilus Regulus and Manlius Vulso were sent with two hundred and thirty war galleys to Africa. They met the Carthaginian navy at Cape Ecnomus and defeated it, and then Regulus landed in Africa with fifteen thousand men.

Carthage had in the meantime engaged a Spartan mercenary

captain, called Xanthippus, to take command of its land forces. At the Battle of Bagradas, Xanthippus using an encircling movement, utterly destroyed the Roman army and took Regulus prisoner. To make things worse for Rome the fleet fell into a storm on its way home, and most of it was destroyed.

The Romans, by a great effort, and at a great sacrifice, were able to build a new fleet which put to sea in 254 B.C. Panormus (Palermo) was captured by storm, and the Punic commander who attempted to recover it was heavily defeated outside its gates. In 249 B.C. the Romans besieged Lilybaeum but were unable to capture it. In the same year the consul Claudius Pulcher made a dash for Drepana. Adherbal, the Punic admiral, went out to meet him and by an adroit manoeuvre drove the Roman ships ashore capturing most of them. The war, which had been dragging for thirteen years seemed again to reach a stalement, and Carthage made overtures for peace, unwisely sending Regulus as its ambassador. Regulus instead of pleading for peace made a vehement plea for prosecuting the war with vigour.

In 247 B.C. Carthage gave the command in Sicily to Hamilcar Barca, a scion of the Hamilcar who fell at Himera in 479 B.C. For five years Hamilcar did more or less what he pleased in Sicily carrying one fortified place after the other. By 242 B.C. the third Roman fleet, which was built and equipped from forced loans, put to sea. Drepana and Lilybaeum were invested. Carthage sent a fleet for relieving them, but the Roman admiral, Lutatius Catullus gained a great victory, thanks to the new poles and pikes with which the Roman gallers were equipped.

Carthage, having lost her fleet, and fearing a second invasion of Africa, sued for peace which was granted on the following terms:

a) Carthage was to abandon all claims to Sicily and thus bring to an end her three hundred year old struggle for the island.

b) Carthage agreed to pay a war indemnity of 3,300 talents within ten years.

The success of the Romans was in a large measure due to their ability to learn from their mistakes, and their determination. Every setback acted as a further incentive to re-doubled efforts. But the Carthaginians also contributed to their own defeat. Since the beginning of the fifth century Carthage had become an oligarchy of wealthy merchants relying for its defence on its navy and on a large body of hired mercenaries to fight its battles. Its manpower was limited. Before the rise of Rome, both Carthage and the Greeks in Sicily engaged mercenaries by the thousand. In her wars with Rome, Carthage found herself pitted against a patriotic citizen army with no mercenaries and an abundance of manpower to more than make up for unfortunate losses.

In 238 B.C. Rome seized Corsica and Sardinia, and Carthage was powerless to contest her action.

The Second Punic War

Hamilcar Barca, in order to compensate for the loss of Sicily, Corsica and Sardinia, obtained a commission from the Carthaginian oligarchy to extend Carthaginian dominion over Spain. Spain at the time was occupied by split tribal units of Ligurians and Celts. The country was rich in copper and silver mines.

Hamilcar's expedition was very successful and the finances of Carthage were soon restored. Hamilcar's real aim however was not so much to restore the crippled finances of Carthage, as to obtain a large recruiting area. He realized that Rome won the First Punic War because of her unlimited manpower. The Iberians were a sturdy, virile race capable of great physical endurance; they fought with deadly thrusting swords, and Hamilcar levied troops among them by conscription.

Massilia (modern Marseilles), a Greek foundation in South Gaul, had great commercial interests in Spain, which the expansion of Carthage jeopardized. She appealed to Rome against the rising power of Carthage in Spain. The Senate sent an embassy to Hamilcar, who protested to the envoys that he was looking for sources of revenue in order to enable Carthage to pay the war indemnity owed to Rome, and promised to protect Saguntum, a Massilian colony south of the Ebro on the east coast of Spain. A second Roman embassy entered into an agreement with Hasdrubal, Hamilcar's son-in-law and successor, whereby the River Ebro was fixed as the boundary between the Roman and Carthaginian spheres of influence.

Hasdrubal died in 221 B.C. and was succeeded by Hannibal, Hamilcar's son. In the following year Hannibal quarrelled with Saguntum and made preparations for its siege. Rome sent envoys asking him to desist, but Hannibal refused and argued that Saguntum lay south of the Ebro. In this he was upheld by the oligarchy

44

at Carthage. Saguntum was captured and sacked in 219 B.C. Rome demanded the surrender of Hannibal, but when Carthage refused, Rome declared war (218 B.C.).

No sooner had Rome declared war on Carthage than Hannibal moved with great alacrity against Italy, in order to prevent Rome from putting its plan into operation, namely a direct attack on Carthage. Hannibal moved with fifty thousand men, forced the passage of the Rhone and crossed the Alps with great difficulty, losing almost half his men and most of his elephants. He arrived at the Po with only twenty-six thousand men. Cornelius Scipio met Hannibal at the Ticinus, but was forced to fall back on the Apennines. Another Roman army under Sempronius Longus joined that of Scipio and fell on Hannibal at the Trebia. Here Hannibal caught them in an ambush and utterly routed them. Thirty thousand Romans were lost in this battle, and the remainder withdrew to the south. Hannibal then moved on to Lake Trasimene in Central Etruria, modern Tuscany, where he found another Roman army waiting for him. For the second time the Roman army was caught in a mesh, and the bulk of it perished. Hannibal then moved south in order to incite the subject peoples of Rome to revolt. Q. Fabius Maximus, the Roman dictator, refused to give battle to Hannibal but satisfied himself with harassing his forces and preventing him receiving supplies by a war of attrition. This eventually would have embarrassed Hannibal but the Senate and Roman people became impatient, and wanted to remove Hannibal from Italy. A new army of fifty thousand men was raised and entrusted to the consuls Aemilius Paullus and Terentius Varro. Hannibal put an army of forty thousand men into the field. The two armies met at Cannae in Southern Italy in 216 B.C. The cavalry was stationed on both wings while the infantry occupied the centre. Hannibal's cavalry chased the Roman cavalry off the battlefield, then wheeled about and encircled the Roman army. Of the fifty thousand Romans, twenty-five thousand were slain, ten thousand were taken prisoners and only fifteen thousand escaped to tell the tale.

After this disaster, Rome adopted the Fabian tactics which were in operation before Cannae. No battle was offered and Hannibal was confined to south Italy where he duly captured Tarentum and Capua but just as quickly lost them. Hannibal badly needed reinforcements which were not forthcoming. The Romans proceeded to contain Hannibal in south Italy and slowly closed the mesh around him. When Hasdrubal, Hannibal's younger brother, arrived in 207 B.C. in North Italy with reinforcements he was cornered at the Metaurus River by the consuls Claudius Nero and Livius and his army was destroyed. His head was tossed into Hannibal's camp. Hannibal, dejected, retired to the hills of Bruttium in the toe of Italy.

The Scipios were sent to Spain to keep the Carthaginian troops engaged, so as to prevent reinforcements from being sent to Italy. The two elder Scipios perished, but the younger Scipio resumed the offensive and captured Carthago Nova. In 205 he returned to Rome and, after a great deal of argument, bickering and recrimination, the Senate conceded to him two legions with which to attack Carthage. Scipio picked two other legions in Sicily and sailed for Africa. He landed at Utica in 204 B.C. After an initial night skirmish with Carthaginians and allied troops, Carthage sued for peace, at the same time recalling Hannibal from Italy.

Scipio's terms for peace were the following: First, Carthage was to cede Spain to Rome; secondly the Carthaginian Navy was to be reduced to twenty galleys, and thirdly Carthage was to pay an indemnity of five thousand talents. The Carthaginian Senate was on the point of accepting the terms, when Hannibal arrived at the crucial moment just as the treaty was about to be signed. Hannibal harangued the Carthaginian Senate into repudiating the pact and resisting. He then took charge of the military operations, and made his preparations to meet the Roman army. The two armies met at Zama Regia, in 202 B.C. The battle was initiated by a mass attack of elephants sent by Hannibal. The infantry of the two sides then interlocked. In the meantime the Roman cavalry drove the Punic cavalry off the battle-field and then wheeled round to destroy the Carthaginian infantry which found itself in a closed mesh. It was Cannae with the tables turned. The Carthaginian army was destroyed, and at this stage even Hannibal counselled Carthage to sue for peace.

The new peace terms were even harsher than the first. In addition to the loss of Spain, Carthage had to pay an indemnity of ten thousand talents, its fleet was reduced to ten galleys, and what was more humiliating, Carthage was not to wage war in

Africa without first obtaining permission from Rome.

The Third Punic War

The last condition brought about the Third Punic War and the final destruction of the city.

Masinissa, the king of Numidia who was an ally of Rome, proceeded after the Second Punic War to encroach on the territory of Carthage and at the same time to cultivate the friendship of Rome by sending her free supplies of wheat, and contingents of troops and elephants to help her in her wars in Europe.

Carthage sent repeated protests to Rome against Masinissa's encroachments, but they fell on deaf ears. Exasperated, the Carthaginians declared war on Masinissa. Although defeated by Masinissa, Carthage became the target of Cato's accusations in the Roman Senate, which finally declared war in 149 B.C. Carthage frantically bid for peace. Whatever conditions were placed by Rome, were immediately accepted by Carthage, only to find that Rome had changed her mind and imposed harsher terms. The final demand of Rome which Carthage would not accept, was that the Carthaginians should abandon their city and settle inland. The Romans besieged the city in 149 B.C., made a breach in the outer wall in 147 B.C. and finally reached the Citadel in 146 B.C. after bitter street fighting. The fifty thousand Carthaginians who surrendered were sold into slavery. The city was razed to the ground and salt was spread over it. A curse was made against anyone who would rebuild it. With the destruction of Carthage, Phoenician power overseas collapsed.

CHAPTER IV
Culture

The foregoing pages were intended to give the reader a short survey of the political history of Phoenicia in order to prepare him for a discussion of the culture of the country. It is now proposed to project against that historical background, the Phoenician cultural achievement, stressing the role of Phoenicia in the invention of the alphabet and its introduction into Europe, the political and social institutions of the nation, the religion of ancient Phoenicia, its industry, commerce and trade, and finally a detailed discussion of its art.

Language

The Phoenician language is a Semitic dialect which, together with Aramaic and Hebrew, developed out of Akkadian, the Semitic language spoken in Mesopotamia from the Third Millennium to the conquest of the country by the Arabs. The spoken language of Phoenicia was already fully developed in the fifteenth century B,C. as we know from the Ras Shamra tablets.

Although the Phoenicians are now universally acknowledged to be the inventors of the alphabet (or rather two alphabets), the number of inscriptions that have come down to us in the cursive script of Byblos are very few indeed, and hardly any literature in the cursive alphabet of Byblos exists.

That such a literature existed, however, and how rich it must have been, we know from the uniformity of the style of the few inscriptions that have come down to us. But the destruction of Sidon by Esarhaddon in the seventh century B.C. and again by Artaxerxes III in the fourth century B.C., and the sack of Tyre by Alexander must have destroyed most of the archives written on papyrus in those cities. What codices existed at Byblos must also have been relegated to oblivion by the wanton destruction of the city at the hands of Aziru in the fourteenth century B.C. Since the sack of the city by Aziru, Byblos indeed came to hold a third place among the cities of Phoenicia, its place being taken by Sidon and Tyre.

However, we do have some literature written in the cuneiform alphabet which was invented at Ras Shamra-Ugarit sometime during the fifteenth century B.C. and a most interesting, illuminating and rich literature it has proved to be. It leads us to deplore the more the loss of the literature of Byblos, Sidon and Tyre and brings home, as nothing else can, the great gap left in our knowledge by the loss of the literature of these three cities. That such literature existed we know from Philo of Byblos who quotes passages from a great Beirut author called Sanchoniathon, who flourished in the twelfth century B.C. References to the celebrated unnamed poets of Tyre and Sidon are to be found in the book of Isaiah.

We now have no less than fifteen inscriptions carved on stone in the Phoenician alphabet, which was soon adopted by all the neighbouring Semitic states. The earliest is that of Ahiram, and the latest that of Bodashtart King of Sidon, besides the inscriptions on Phoenician coins struck in Phoenicia, Tarsus, Carthage and their dependencies. Most of these inscriptions in fact were discovered outside Phoenicia.

The literature of Ras Shamra includes hymns, myths and legends, of a high literary merit, as well as a treatise on veterinary medicine, wills, accounts, bills, inventories of goods and so forth. In the hymns of Ras Shamra-Ugarit we find the origin of some of the best hymns in the Old Testament with the name of Baal in place of that of Jahweh. This fact has led many scholars to conclude that both the hymns in the Old Testament and those of Ras Shamra were derived from still more ancient Semitic literature and which inspired the later literature of the Israelites and other Semitic tribes of the Middle East. It is not intended here to cumber the reader with the interesting literature retrieved by Dr. Schaeffer and published by Virolleand, Dussaud, Nougayrol and others, but it would be appropriate to cite a few examples, taken from Obermann's *Ugaritic Mythology*, published by Yale University Press,

Hymns Invitation to Anat

> "*Ye (shall) put a gem on her breast:*
> *As a token of the love of Aliyan Baal,*
> *Of the loyal(ty) ? of Pidriya, daughter of Ar,*
> *Of the devotion of Tilliya, daughter of Rabb,*

Of the love of Arsiya, daughter of Ya'buddar.
Like stewards then do ye enter:
At the feet of Anat crouch ye and fall down,
Prostrate yourselves and honor her.
And proclaim ye to the Virgin Anath,
Declare to the Yamamat of the People:
(Thus) spoke Aliyan Baal,
(Thus) said Aliy Qardam:
'Strike thou the warriors to the ground,
Put to the dust the repellers,
Pour out submission to the core of the earth,
Overwhelm insurrection to the core of the land.

Let thy compassion (for me) constrain thee:
Let it unite thee with me.
Thy feet shall gallop toward me,
Thy tread shall stamp out impudence.
I have (at heart) a thing I wish to tell thee,
A matter I wish to convey to thee,
(It's) a thing about wood,
And a secret about stone.
(It's) the contention of heaven with the earth,
Of the deep with the stars.
(It's) a stone of splendor, which the heavens have not known,
A thing that men have not known,
And the multitudes of the earth have not perceived.
(It concerns) a monument that I do desire,
Amid the mountain of mine, God of Sapon,
In Holiness, on the mount of my inheritance,
In Delight, on the hill of Endeavor.'"

Anath Threatens her Father, who appeases her

"Rejoice not, rejoice not! . . .
I shall wou(nd the crown) of thy scalp!
I shall make (thy) gray hair flow (with blood),
Thy gray beard with gore!"

Baal Destroys a Rival with a Weapon made by Hayin

"The Skilful one — a staff he fashions,
And pronounces its design:
'Thy name, yea thine, is "He-Will-Expel! He-Will-Expel!"
Let him expel Sea!
Let him expel Sea from his throne,
River, from the seat of his reign!
Thou shalt swoop in the hand of Baal,
Like a vulture in his fingers!
Let him strike Prince Sea on the shoulder,
Between the arms, Chieftain River!'

Swoops the staff in the hand of Baal,
Like a vulture in his fingers.
He strikes Prince Sea on the shoulder,
Between the arms, Chieftain River.

Sea has withstood,
He does not bend,
His hips do not quiver,
His figure does not waver.

The Skilful one — a staff he fashions,
And pronounces its design:
'Thy name, yea thine, is "Ah, He-Will-Force-Out!
Ah, He-Will-Force-Out!"
Let him force out Sea!
Let him force out Sea from his throne,
River, from the seat of his reign!
Thou shalt swoop in the hand of Baal,
Like a vulture in his fingers!
Let him strike Prince Sea on the head,
Between the eyes, Chieftain River!
Then will Sea sink down
And will fall to the ground.'

Now swoops the staff in the hand of Baal,
Like a vulture in his fingers.

He strikes Prince Sea on the head,
Between the eyes, Chieftain River.

Sea sinks down,
He falls to the ground,
His hips do quiver,
And his figure does waver.
(Now) Baal routs and deranges Sea,
He destroys Chieftain River into ruin."

The Legend of King Keret [1]

Keret, the King of Sidon, was entrusted by El, the father of the gods, with the command of an army to march against the Terachites, who invaded Canaan and captured five cities. Keret dreaded the venture; he was seized with great fear and shut himself up in his house weeping. El appeared to Keret in his dream and promised him a son. Keret got up, and went to fight the Terachites, after having made the necessary sacrifices. He drove the Terachites back and proceeded south. The King of Edom bought him off with some presents and Keret married the grand-daughter of the King of Edom. The words of King Keret asking for Mesheb-Hory the grand daughter of the King of Edom are worth quoting. Here is a translation:

"Give me Mesheb-Hory, who is the grace of the issue of the eldest son. Her charm is like the charm of Anat. Her beauty is like the beauty of Ashtart, her eyelids are blossoms of lapis lazuli, that I may bask in the glance of her eyes." [2]

We shall have occasion to give more examples of Phoenician literature when we come to discuss Phoenician religion. Of the texts that have come down to us in the cursive Phoenician script which reached its full development at Byblos, the earliest example we have is the inscription on the sarcophagus of Ahiram, the King of Byblos who lived in the thirteenth century B.C. and was a contemporary of Rameses II. [3]

---

[1] Condensed from Schaeffer: *The Cuneiform Texts of Ras Shamra.*
[2] From Schaeffer: *loc. cit.*
[3] Some historians prefer a later date to this.

This script evolved out of an earlier Semitic script which is known as the proto-Sinaitic script discovered at Sarabit el Khadem in Sinaii. The proto-Sinaitic script in turn developed from some Egyptian hieroglyphic letters and others which were suggested by acrophony: that is, the representation of a letter by the picture of some subject the first letter of which starts with that letter. Thus the letter B is represented by a house 𐤁 which is *beth* in practically all Semitic languages; the letter D ▢ is represented by a door, which is *daleth* in most Semitic languages; the letter A is represented by an ox' head, which is *aleph* in most Semitic languages, and so on. Dr. Albright has recently attempted a decipherment and a translation of this script which is gaining acceptance among scholars. [1] The Byblos cursive script is a stylization and standardization of this script. Thus the ox head is standardized thus ⊄ for *aleph* or A, the house is represented ᓄ for *beth* or B and the door is represented thus ᓄ for *daleth* or D. It is not certain how long a period elapsed between the proto-Sinaitic script of Sarabit el Khadem in Sinaii and the script used on the sarcophagus of Ahiram of Byblos. We venture to suggest that the cuneiform alphabet of Ras Shamra was invented first, but having proved very cumbersome, a substitute script, modelled on that of Egypt, was experimented with in the fifteenth century B.C. and was slowly standardized in the course of the next two centuries at Byblos. It may here be added that a third still indecipherable script, perhaps syllabic, was in use for a short time at Byblos during the fifteenth-fourteenth centuries but was probably discarded in favour of the script which was developed from the proto-Sinaitic script.

Let us now probe into the identity of the man who carved the proto-Sinaitic script. Sarabit el Khadem in Sinaii is an extensive quarry containing copper ore and turquoise. The quarries have inscriptions on the walls which give the names of the Pharoahs during whose reign the mines were opened; all of these belong to the Eighteenth Dynasty (c.1580-1321 B.C.). Nearby there were other mines at a place called Wadi el Maghara which were exploited in earlier periods. Thus the mines of Sarabit el Khadem are later.

We know that in antiquity Byblos supplied Egypt with the

[1] Cf. Bulletin of the American School of Oriental Research, No. 109.

timber she needed, and in exchange the Phoenician city received granite, syenite, turquoise and copper. Would it be too much to suggest that one of the kings of Byblos in the fifteenth century B.C. sent an emissary to supervise the quarrying and transport of the stone for his master? In Byblos, the chief deity was *Baalat Gebal*, or the Lady of Byblos. In the inscription at Sarabit el Khadem, the name of Baalat is clearly legible. We venture to suggest that the *Baalat* mentioned in the Sarabit el Khadem inscription is identical with the *Baalat* of Gebal, and that the Gibelite labourers and overseers wished to venerate their great deity away from home. In a stele set up by Yahumelek, King of Byblos during the Persian Period, *Baalat Gebal* is represented wearing a sun-disk between two horns, the headdress of the Egyptian cow-goddess Hathor. At Sarabit el Khadem next to the proto-Sinaitic inscription, there is a decipherable invocation in Egyptian hieroglyphs addressed to Hathor. May we suggest that the two inscriptions are contemporary and were carved by a Gibelite, a Phoenician from Byblos who was versed in the two languages?

The Political and Social Institutions of Phoenicia

Like most Semitic city-states, each city before the twelfth century B.C. was governed by an hereditary king, whose will was absolute, and who combined the functions of judge, commander and high-priest. With the arrival of the Aegeans and the fusion of the local Semitic Canaanites with the new comers, new political notions and ideas were introduced. We know from Sir Arthur Evans' excavations at Knossos and Professor Alan Wace's excavations at Mycenae that there was some sort of court life in the Aegean. We venture to suggest that the courtiers were an exclusive class of rich men who were consulted, formally or informally, by the king. The King of Knossos was a merchant king, and he no doubt would from time to time consult the leading merchants, or a panel of them, on important state and business matters. In historic Greece, every city had its *Beule* or *Gerusia*, a Council of elders, which they probably adopted from the earlier pre-Hellenic Aegeans.

From the twelfth century B.C. on, it seems that the newcomers brought with them the political ideas of their countries and introduced them into Phoenicia. We learn from the Bible that there was at Byblos an assembly of Elders, or Senate, which gave advice to the King. In Carthage we know from Greek and Latin literature that there was a Senate consisting of 100 persons. The origin of these Senates, we venture to suggest, is to be sought in the Aegean stratum in the Phoenician population. Although there is no evidence that such Councils of Elders existed in the twelfth century B.C. there is incontrovertible evidence that they existed from the sixth century B.C. and later, in Tyre, Sidon, Byblos and Aradus. Their power seems to have grown with time. By the Persian period, they seem to have become so powerful as to overrule the king in many matters.

The rest of the population consisted of free men and slaves. The free men engaged in husbandry, fishing and trade, leaving the onerous tasks of actual ploughing, rowing and other menial duties to slaves.

Carthage never had a king but only a *shofet* or judge who presided over the Senate. The aristocracy of Carthage was an aristocracy of wealth and not of lineage. In her later days, Tyre dispensed with royalty and modelled her constitution on that of her daughter city Carthage, by electing an annual *shofet*.

The armies of Phoenician cities were mercenaries, stiffened by a selected corps of citizens. One of the chief causes of the collapse of Carthage was her reliance on mercenaries to fight her battles.

Religion

Thanks to Dr. Schaeffer's excavations of Ras Shamra-Ugarit and to the mine of information which the tablets that he discovered there have yielded on the religion of the Phoenicians, we are now better informed about the religion, not only of the Phoenicians, but of most of the Semitic countries west of the Syrian desert. The role that religion plays in the culture of any nation cannot be over-emphasized. It affects its literature, it inspires and moulds its art, it is the basis and foundation of its legal and moral code, it moulds and fashions its very existence.

In the library of King Niqmad at Ras Shamra-Ugarit, Dr. Schaeffer found and is still finding numerous tablets which deal with religious matters. "By far the majority of the tablets from the Ras Shamra library deal with religious matters," says Dr. Schaeffer. The tablets include magical rites and formulae which were destined to ensure fertility. These rites together with the terra cotta figurines of the goddess of fertility, whose sexual organs were made very prominent so that their function might be better performed in nature, reflect a belief in sympathetic magic. Further Dr. Schaeffer pointed out the connection between the fertility cult and the cult of the dead. The dead needed sustenance and this was provided by means of offerings in the form of libations and food. Dr. Schaeffer further drew attention to the fact that the same idea was found among the Mycenaeans and other nations of the past.

The Canaanites, like the Egyptians and their brethren, the Babylonians, had their pantheon, which was retained later by the Phoenicians. At the head of the pantheon stood *El*, who was the supreme deity, the king of the gods, and whose will was irrevocable. On one of the stele at Ras Shamra he is represented seated on a throne; his symbol of strength is the bull; he is the sun-god.

Asherah of the sea was the wife of *El*, but judging by the Ras Shamra texts *El* was by no means a faithful husband. *Asherah* was the counsellor of the gods, but gave her counsel only when she was asked. *El* and *Asherah* of the sea may not be invoked directly but through an intermediary god or goddess.

Baal was the son of *El* and *Ashirat-Yam*. He was identified with the Egyptian *Set* or *Sutekh*, the Hittite *Teshub*, the Phoenician *Reshef*, and the Aramaean *Hadad*. He was the god of thunder, rain and storm. He is always represented carrying a thunderbolt ending in a spear. His symbol is the bull, and he was imbued with the same strength as his father.

Proto-Phoenician or Canaanite mythology revolves around the death and resurrection of *Baal*. *Baal* went forth to fight on the edge of the desert, where he encountered bull-headed beasts with human bodies. A duel developed and *Baal* was overcome and slain. *Baal* had no temple dedicated to him, so *Ashirat-Yam* pleaded with *El* to have a temple erected to him. *Hijon*, the god of craftsmanship, fashioned a throne with a footstool and a table and presented them to *El*, who granted permission for the construction of a temple to *Baal*. To those familiar with Greek mythology,[1] the parallels between Greek and Canaanite religion cannot pass unnoticed.

The gods then proceeded to build the temple under the supervision of *Latpon*.

Kousor was a sea-god who controlled the seasons, and has his opposite number among the Greek gods in *Poseidon*.

[1] Cf. Seltman: *The Twelve Olympians.*

Aliyan was the son of *Baal* whose duty was to watch over and control the springs and underground waters. He also represented the growth of plants. *Baal* and *Aliyan* ruled over the earth during the autumn, winter and spring, the time of sewing, germination and growth, while *Mot* ruled during the summer, the period of reaping and harvest. [1]

A yearly struggle took place between *Aliyan* and *Mot* which corresponds to the agricultural cycle. The struggle started in spring when *Baal* in aid of his son *Aliyan* hurls thunderbolts and sends torrential rains, storms and tempests over Phoenicia. However *Mot* eventually emerged victorious and first *Baal*, then *Aliyan* were killed by *Mot* ushering in the warm summer months.

"Baal descends into the womb of the earth, and the fruit of the trees are subject to the intense heat of the sun."

Aliyan, in the form of fruit, carried on the unequal struggle alone, but he too eventually succumbed and was forced to go and join his father. Before he did that, he indulged in a bout of sexual orgy.

"He makes love seventy-seven times."
"He makes love eighty-eight times." [2]

Anat, *Aliyan*'s sister and mistress, went searching for her lover in every field and pasture.

Anat eventually arrived at the abode of the dead inside the earth and found the body of *Aliyan*. She carried it to the heights of Saphon, where she buried him, and sacrificed to him. She then sought out *Mot*, and implored him to restore *Aliyan* to life but he refused. She lay hold of *Mot* and killed him.

"Anat seized Mot, the divine son,
"With a sickle she cut him,
"With a winnow she winnows him,
"With fire she scorches him,
"With a mill she crushes him,
"She scatters his flesh in the field to be eaten by birds,
"So that his destiny may be fulfilled." [3]

---

[1] According to some scholars *Aliyan-Baal* is not the son of *Baal* but *Baal* himself. *Aliyan*, which means high, is explained as an epithet.
[2] From Obermann: *Ugaritic Mythology.*
[3] From Obermann: *loc. cit.*

This was merely the harvest rite translated into mythology. Eventually *Aliyan* was brought back to life, to start the agricultural cycle again.

Besides this myth which was the common property of all Semites in some form or another, each Phoenician city had its favourite deity. Byblos had its *Baal-Reshef* and its *Baalat Gebal*. Sidon had its *Eshmun-Adonis*, a form of *Aliyan*. Tyre had its *Melqart*. Aradus had its *Baal-Yam*, a form of Poseidon. *Ashtart*, the goddess of love and fertility was worshipped everywhere. In some cases she played the role of *Anat*, but without her redeeming virtue of constancy in love. In fact, *Ashtart* was, in character, the very antithesis of *Anat*, and promiscuity was the key-note of her life. This is quite natural in a goddess of fertility, at a time when belief in sympathetic magic was very strong. Promiscuity and breeding among human beings was supposed to influence animals and crops, and raise in them a similar desire, and induce the seeds sown to fertilize and produce.

Religion and fertility were so interwoven among the Semites and the dwellers of the Nile Valley. In Babylonia the role of *Ashtart* was played by *Ishtar* and the role of *Aliyan-Eshmun-Adonis* was played by *Tammuz* or *Dumuzi*. In Egypt the role of *Aliyan* was played by *Osiris*, the role of *Mot* by *Sutekh* and the role of the bereaved wife or mistress by *Isis*. The fertility cult originated in Mesopotamia in remote antiquity, and from there spread into Syria, Phoenicia and Egypt, varying slightly in form but not in essentials.

Trade and Commerce

The Phoenicians, (the nation which came into being as a result of the fusion of the Canaanites, the aborigines of the country whom we may call proto-Phoenicians, and the Aegeans), stepped into the gap left by the disruption of the Aegean world, and inherited the thalassocracy which was vacated by the Achaeans and their kindred peoples. As we explained above the new race of mariners were not entirely ignorant of the waters through which they plied, partly from the Aegean side of their ancestry and partly from the fact that they were seamen from time immemorial. However, in earlier days, that is, before the twelfth century B.C., they plied between Phoenicia and Egypt. There is even no evidence that they reached Cyprus before that time, as Cyprus was controlled by the Aegeans, and it would have been extremely hazardous for the proto-Phoenicians to navigate in their own ships in Cypriote waters. What trade there was, before the twelfth century B.C., and it was considerable, was carried by Aegeans with a Mycenaean culture.

The Aegean thalassocracy having come to an end in the twelfth century there was no limit to Phoenician maritime expansion. World marine trade became their monopoly. They carried the products of Egypt, Babylonia, Assyria and Syria to the Greek world, to North Africa, to Sicily, to Spain, and even to the remote coast of Etruria.

The Dorians who invaded Greece in the twelfth century were strictly speaking a land force. They had not yet learnt to take advantage of the harbours and havens with which nature had favoured the Aegean basin, nor had they mastered the craft of seamanship. Being still in a barbaric state, unable to produce, yet fully appreciating the refined products of the east, they allowed, and perhaps encouraged Phoenician traders to display their wares in their own country, in order to buy their goods. The Phoenicians thus penetrated the Greek world and established trading stations at Corinth, Thera, Kythera and Thasos to mention a few places. At Corinth a Semitic deity called Melikertes was worshipped which could only have been introduced by the Tyrians. The etymological relationship between Melkart, the patron deity of Tyre and Melikertes is obvious. At Imbros and Samothrace, the Kabeiroi were worshipped; they were none other than the Kebirim or "The Great Ones", of the Phoenicians. The *Iliad* and the *Odyssey* speak of the trade of the Sidonians and Phoenicians, and of the fine products which they brought to the Aegean.

For three long centuries the Phoenicians held full and undisputed sway over the Mediterranean Sea and its offshoots, the Aegean and Tyrrhenian seas. Their main trade, however, was with Greece. Greece during this period had nothing to offer to the Phoenicians for the articles of luxury which they brought with them but precious metals and slaves. The Semites showed such a strong predilection for blue-eyed fair haired Greek damsels, that when they could not get those precious objects of their heart's desire by trade, they generally abducted them. Herodotus states that such an abduction was the cause of the Persian wars but this of course was one of the slight exaggerations of the great "Father of History".

With the marine lore which they acquired from the Aegeans the Phoenicians made use of their knowledge of the stars in navigation; they learnt astronomy from the Babylonians; thus they were able to travel in uncharted seas with the stars to guide them.

By the eighth century, however, the new inhabitants of Greece had come to learn of the favours with which nature endowed their new home and proceeded to take advantage of them. They started building ships and competing with the Phoenicians first in their own home waters of the Aegean, and later, farther afield in Sicily, South Italy and even in Egypt. They learnt astronomy from the Phoenicians and about its benefits and use in navigation, and soon entered into competition with the Phoenicians on the high seas and outstripped them. The method used by the Greeks in their commercial struggle with the Phoenicians was flagrant piracy. By degrees the Phoenicians were forced to retire from the Aegean, and to seek outlets for their trade and commerce in the Western Mediterranean.

The period of the decline of Phoenician trade in the Aegean corresponded more or less with the rise of Assyria and the loss of Phoenician independence. There were thus more than one cause for the adventurous foundation of Carthage; loss of independence at home and loss of trade in the Aegean. The focus of interest now centred on Carthage. The Carthaginians established trading stations at Cadiz in Spain, at Panormus (Palermo) in Sicily, and at various other places in Sardinia, Corsica, Malta and Gozo. We have followed the struggle that Carthage entered into with the Greeks in Sicily. Against the Greeks, Carthage more than maintained her position, but she succumbed after a heroic and unequal struggle with Rome. For by the time Rome had entered the arena of Western Mediterranean policies, Carthage, through the acquisition of wealth, had become an effeminate city of wealth-seeking merchants, and lost those virile traits of adventure and hardihood which led its early settlers to bring about its foundation.

> *"Ill fares the land, to hastening ills a prey,*
> *Where wealth accumulates and men decay"*

The Golden Age of Phoenicia, between the eleventh and

eighth centuries B.C. was brought to an end by the Assyrian invasion. However, the glory of Phoenicia was only dimmed but not
completely eclipsed. The Phoenicians still carried the trade from
their ports to Egypt, North Africa and the West, and continued
to reap immense gain for their labour; but their profits were shared,
in the form of tribute, by that "silent partner" the King of Assyria.
No wonder then that we often find the Pheonician cities in revolt
against the yoke of Assyria. The Assyrian yoke, and its successor
the yoke of Babylonia, were very irksome. On the one hand, it
crippled the trade of Phoenicia, and on the other took the lion's
share from the profits of the Phoenicians. The fall of Niniveh in
612 B.C. and later the fall of Babylon in 538 B.C. were hailed with
rejoicing by Tyre and Sidon. The rise of Persia, which promised
the liberation of the subject races, was as welcome as the advent
of the allies to Syria, Lebanon, Iraq and Palestine in 1917. But
just as the empty promises of the allies in that year proved a great
disappointment for the "liberated" countries, in like manner, the
mild and tolerant rule of Cyrus and Darius I were to be the har-
bingers of a yoke just as irksome as that of a Sennacherib or a
Nebuchadrezzar. Phoenician trade flourished at the outset and to
the Phoenicians were promised the glories of a better day. The
King of Sidon was an ally of Persia and Admiral of the Persian
fleet. Under the later harem-ridden Achaemaenids and the covetous
rapacity of their semi-independent satraps, the Phoenicians found
themselves in just the same position as under the Assyrians and
Babylonians. They continued to carry the marine trade of the
ancient world, but what they kept for their labours, after paying
tribute to the great king and his greedy satraps, was hardly worth-
while. No wonder then that we see Tyre and Sidon, Aradus
(Arvad) and Tripoli ranged with either the rebellious satraps, or
taking sides with Egypt, even if the act involved the destruction of
their city. No wonder that most Phoenician cities opened their
gates to Alexander, except Tyre, which resisted only because she
wished to remain neutral in a struggle the outcome of which
seemed uncertain, and not because of any loyalty towards Persia.
The fact that Sidon readily submitted to Alexander greatly influenced Tyre in making her decision to resist, on account of the
rivalry between the two cities.

Under the Hellenistic monarchies, Phoenicia again held her

own. Marine trade, it is true, was no longer a Phoenician monopoly, for Rhodes shared the trade with Phoenicia and perhaps carried the greater part of it, and Alexandria became the emporium of world trade, yet the great admirals of the day were Phoenicians; Philocles, the admiral of Demetrius Poliorcetes, was a Tyrian. The Phoenician cities flourished first under the Ptolemies, and later when they became autonomous under the late Seleucids. The Greek world was no longer closed to them, and the new transfusion of Aryan blood, this time of Greeks and Macedonians, added virility to the nation. Hellenized they became, but not altogether oblivious of their heritage. During the Roman Period, Phoenicians and Greeks made the bulk of the tradesmen of the Roman Empire. The Phoenicians remained a nation of great seamen and shipbuilders until the beginning of the present century when they became unable to compete with the steam ships produced on the Clyde and on the Humber, on account of the lack of steel and other raw materials to cope with the requirements of the industry of the nineteenth and twentieth centuries of our era.

Industry

The Phoenicians traded mainly in the products which were manufactured by others and not by themselves; their own industry was very limited in extent. Indeed they would have been hard put to it if they relied for their trade on their own products. It was the unlimited produce of the hinterland from the Lebanon to the Persian Gulf that they carried over the seas to Egypt, Greece, Cyprus, Africa, Spain and the Islands in the basin of the western Mediterranean and brought back the products of the latter countries to Phoenicia whence they were carried by Aramaeans to the hinterland of Asia. However, they did have a small industry which was fostered by their rulers.

The excavations at Byblos have revealed that the jeweller's craft achieved a very high level in Phoenicia, although it could not compete with the Egyptian or Babylonian jewellery nor free itself completely from their influence.

From time immemorial Phoenicia supplied fish to the hinterland, and the fishing industry was developed at a very early date during the Neolithic Period, judging by the number of bone fish hooks which were discovered in large numbers in the Neolithic level at Byblos.

Ship-building was perhaps their second chief industry, which however took first place during the Golden Age of Phoenicia. With the forests of Lebanon immediately behind, timber was at hand. Phoenicia even before the twelfth century B.C. built ships in its yards for itself as well as for Egypt.

An industry which gave world-wide fame to Phoenicia was the purple and crimson dye which was extracted from the murex shell. The cloth which was produced in Syria or Egypt was dyed in special vats along the Phoenician coast and re-exported. Among the theories advanced for their name is that which seeks to associate it with the colour of the dye they produced. *Phoinikes*, in Greek means red. The fame of this dye continued even into the Byzantine Period.

Glass was invented in Phoenicia sometime in the Late Bronze Age. Glazed paste or faience was known in Egypt and Mesopotamia, but translucent moulded glass is an invention of the Phoenicians and the secret was kept by the Phoenicians till the beginning of the Christian era. A Sidonian invented blown glass in the first century A.D., and from Sidon it passed to Capua and Gaul.

Ivory carving was practised at a very early date. Examples of it were discovered at Ras Shamra, Byblos and Sidon. Solomon and Ahab introduced Phoenician craftsmen to decorate their palaces with carved ivory panels, while the famous ivory panels discovered at Arslan Tash (ancient Til Barsip) betray Phoenician workmanship.

Besides these main industries, husbandry flourished only to a small extent, being circumscribed by the limited amount of land at the disposal of Phoenician cities. In addition Phoenicia produced pottery, bronze implements and weapons. Figurines, coins and other minor industries will be discussed in the following section.

Art

Phoenicia, lying as it does athwart the caravan routes and martial highways of the past, between the great empires of antiquity, was strongly influenced by their art. She borrowed freely from Egypt, Mesopotamia and the Aegean. Just as the nation itself after the twelfth century B.C. was the result of a fusion of two races, so its art is the outcome of the juxtaposition of the art of Egypt, Babylonia, Cappadocia and the Aegean. In some cases Phoenician artists freely copied models of Babylonian and

Egyptian art; in others they adapted and juxtaposed. Of the two great proto-Phoenician cities so far excavated, Byblos has shown strong tendencies to model its art on that of Egypt while Ras Shamra was more influenced by its neighbours the Aegeans and Mesopotamia, but the difference is one of degree only. Both Byblos and Ras Shamra copied and adapted from all and sundry.

As from the twelfth century B.C., Phoenician art was nothing but the natural continuation and development of Aegean art. What the Phoenicians had learnt from Egypt and Mesopotamia was not indeed forgotten, but they clothed their lore in a new garb. The assimilation of the various elements which helped to mould Phoenician art gave rise to a new artistic expression which advanced a long way from its proto-types, and brought about the creation of an art which was as Phoenician as any murex shell on the coast of Tyre and Sidon.

Small Art: Jewellery

The bulk of the treasures and jewels of the proto-Phoenician Canaanites which were retrieved during the last few decades come mainly from the royal cemetery at Byblos. It is fitting at this juncture to recount the story of the discovery of the earliest of these treasures, which is not devoid of interest, and to narrate the romantic tale of the peregrination of another treasure of a contemporary date which was discovered in an unknown locality in Phoenicia, before actually describing the individual works of art included in both caches.

In 1922, a small landslide near the shore at Byblos revealed an ancient hypogeum which was intact. It consisted of a chamber cut in the side of the rock at the bottom of a deep square shaft. Monsieur Virolleand, the Director of the *Services des Antiquités* at the time, undertook the examination of the tomb soon after its discovery. The chamber contained a large stone sarcophagus with a lid provided on the top with four bollard-like supports, one at each corner. The lid was lowered into the shaft by means of ropes tied to the supports. The tomb contained a rich assortment of articles for the use of the deceased in the after life. Amongst other things, Mr. Virolleand discovered a bronze scimitar in the form of a sickle generally called *harpe* in Greek (Pl. 3, a) which was decorated with an uraeus; a cruse in silver with a long spout resembling a modern tea-pot, ribbed vertically down the sides,

PLATE 1 *Jewelry from Byblos ; (top) pendant, (bottom) pectoral, (Beirut National Museum)*

PLATE 2 *Precious objects from Byblos; (top) gold rosette, (bottom) obsidian ointment bottle. (Beirut National Museum)*

PLATE 3   *Precious objects from Byblos; (top)* harpe *dagger, (bottom) silver cruse,*
(Beirut National Museum)

PLATE 4 *Baal of Raṣ Ṣhamra* (*Louvre*)

PLATE 5 *Ivories from Samaria (Palestine Archeological Museum, Jerusalem)*

PLATE 6   *Bronze figurine ; Phoenician Deity (American University of Beirut Museum)*

PLATE 7 *Bronze figurines of Phoenician Deities (American University of Beirut Museum)*

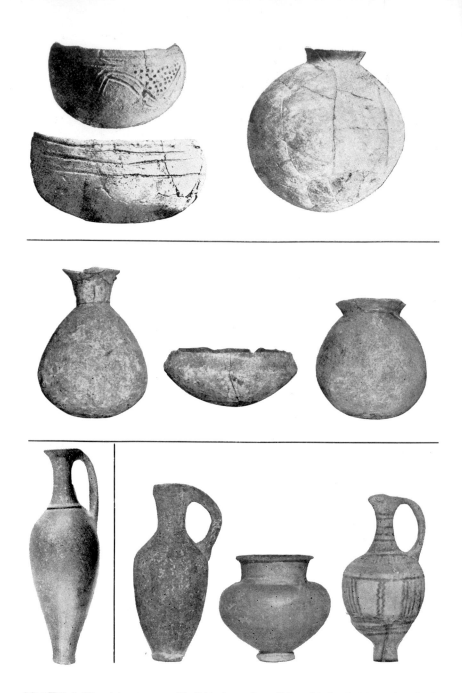

PLATE 8 *Phoenician pottery: Neolithic (top, from Beirut National Museum); Chalcolithic (middle); Early Bronze Age (bottom, left); Middle Bronze Age (Bottom, right) (American University of Beirut Museum) (not to scale)*

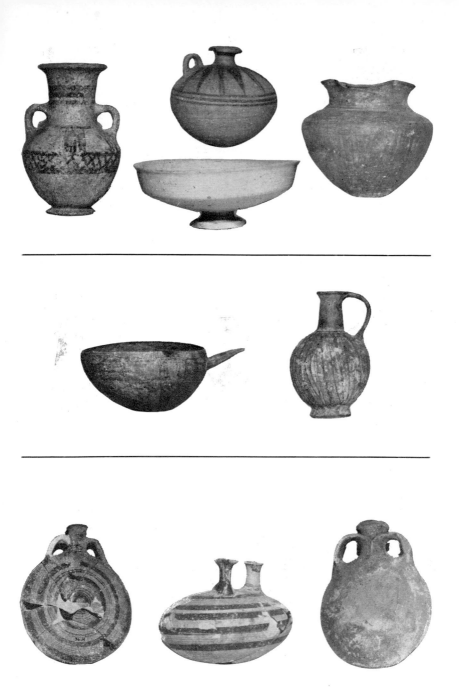

PLATE 9 *Phoenician pottery: Late Bronze Age (top), Base ring ware (middle),
Mycenaean pots and imitation (bottom) (American University of Beirut Museum)
(not to scale)*

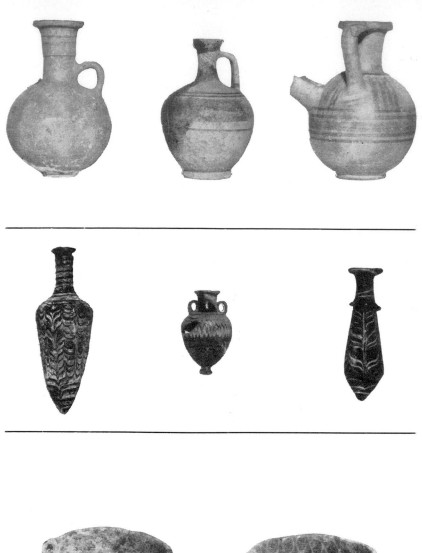

PLATE 10   *Phoenician pottery, Iron Age (top), Phoenician Glass (middle and bottom),*
(American University of Beirut Museum) (not to scale)

(Pl. 3, b) an ointment bottle with a disc cover in obsidian, decorated with gold bands around the rim, at the base and around the lid (Pl. 2, b). The gold band on the cover was carved with the name of Amenemhat III, an Egyptian king of the Twelfth Dynasty (2000-1777 B.C.).

The bronze scimitar betrays Babylonian inspiration, the uraeus is an Egyptian motif, and the form of the silver cruse is Mycenaean. In this single hypogeum we thus perceive the influences which helped to mould proto-Phoenician art concentrated in one and the same spot.

Yet another rich burial was discovered in some unknown locality of Phoenicia by unauthorized persons in a clandestine excavation. The treasure was smuggled into Palestine where it was bought by a local dealer in antiquities who in turn sold it to an eminent archaeologist and historian, who bought it for his institution. The antiquities dealer in Palestine undertook to obtain an export licence from the Palestine authorities and charged the archaeologist with the export fee. However, as the dealer knew only too well that no export permit would be granted for this valuable treasure because of its intrinsic and educational value, he smuggled it out of the country without the knowledge of the archaeologist. In due course the eminent archaeologist published a beautiful gold pectoral, which was included in the collection. By a stroke of fate the person who was head of the Antiquities Department in Palestine at the time resigned and was engaged by the institution which bought the treasure, in the capacity as Field Director. When taking over his duties he was shown the collection and was told that it had been exported from Palestine with the full knowledge of the Department of Antiquities from whom an export licence was obtained. As he was the Acting Director at the time, he did not remember any such export licence being granted. On enquiries being made, he found that no authorization had been issued to permit the export of the collection, and no application was even made for such a permit. The dealer was obliged to return them to Palestine.

When the collection reached Palestine, it became evident to the Department of Antiquities in that country that the collection must have been found in Phoenicia, possibly at Byblos. The *Services des Antiquités* in Lebanon were apprized of the fact and a high ranking official was sent to Jerusalem to examine them. Having satisfied himself that the collection came from Phoenicia, and possibly from Byblos, the official opened negotiations with the dealer for their purchase, and eventually succeeded in restoring them to their home in Lebanon, where together with the other valuable treasures from Byblos they now grace the National Museum of Beirut with their presence, to the delight of scientists and laymen alike.

The objects include a gold pectoral studded with precious stones and decorated with a pair of the eyes of Osiris (*utzat*), a pair of Uraei (the sacred cobra), a pair of cows wearing the golden disc of Ra' between their horns, human figures, together with two cartouches bearing the name of Amenemhat III, and the Egyptian symbol of life, the ankh (Pl. 1, b). The pectoral represents the facade of an Egyptian temple. Although the art is strongly influenced by Egyptian art there are indications that the workmanship is Phoenician. Besides this, there were gold pendants, one in the form of a clam shell with a scarab with outstretched wings attached to it, above which there is a lotus flower a rosette in gold repoussé work (Pl. 2, a), gold bracelets, a gold torque, finger rings, one of which is mounted on a lapis lazuli cylinder seal, and another mounted on a scarab; gold toggle pins; gold bracelets of various sizes, haematite and steatite ointment bottles; gold horse-shoes; alabaster vases; gold vases and a cruse in blue paste decorated with gold bands; a bronze lamp and other objects. [1]

As soon as the first burial treasury was discovered, the authorities in Lebanon realized the great importance of Byblos and decided on the excavation of the site. Monsieur Montet was entrusted with the task in 1923 and opened the campaign with an examination of the ancient cemetery. Monsieur Montet discovered nine other tombs cut in the rock at the bottom of shafts sunk in the rock. Eight of these were contemporary with the first tomb, i.e. belonging to the Twelfth Dynasty (2000-1770 B.C.) while the ninth, that of Ahiram, belongs to the Nineteenth Dynasty (1299-1222 B.C.).

The contents of the first eight tombs were most illuminating.

[1] For a detailed descriptive list of these objects, cf. M. Chéhab: *Un trésor d'orfèvrerie Syro-Egyptien* in Bulletin du Musée de Beyrouth, Vol. I, pp. 7-21.

Amongst other objects, the following important treasures were found:

A gold pendant, resembling the facade of an Egyptian temple and encrusted with semi-precious stones: two royal figures adorn the field, sitting facing each other and wearing the crown of Upper Egypt; between them, hovers a hawk with outstretched wings, while above there is a representation of a winged sun-disc; below the hawk is the symbol of the Horus of gold (Pl. 1, a).

A gold pectoral in the form of a clam shell studded with semi-precious stones and decorated from top to bottom with the sacred scarab, followed by a cartouche bearing the name of Ipshemuabi in Egyptian hieroglyphs, and a hawk with outstretched wings.

Several scimitars of the *harpe* type, one of which bears the name of Ipshemuabi, the king of Byblos, a contemporary of Amenemhat IV; crescent-shaped gold pectorals made in repoussé work, representing a hawk with outstretched wings in the middle, and a hawk's head at either tip of the pectoral; a dagger decorated with a mosaic work; a silver mirror with a handle; an obsidian jewel box, carved with the name of Amenemhat IV, gold finger-rings, bracelets, head-bands and beads complete the rich contents of the tomb.

Although all these objects betray strong Egyptian influence, only a few of them, the obsidian perfume bottle and the obsidian jewel box are of Egyptian workmanship. The remainder are of Phoenician workmanship. This view was expressed by most Egyptologists who see in the objects concerned workmanship inferior to that of the Egyptian craftsmen, and mistakes in the hieroglyphs which could have only been made by an unpractised foreign hand.

In ivory, the Phoenician artists found a happy medium. Fragments of ivory inlay for boxes were found in several places in Phoenicia. The ivories discovered by Dr. Schaeffer at Ras Shamra in 1952 belong to the Late Bronze Age; they probably represent part of the inlay of a royal bed. It is strongly influenced by Egyptian art. In the same place Dr. Schaeffer discovered, in his first campaign, a cover of a jewel box carved with the representation of the goddess of fertility seated on a throne. Her hair is dressed in waves, held in place by a ribbon; except for a necklace, she is naked from the neck to the waist. At the waist she wears a flounced skirt. In either hand she holds ears of corn to two

67

6

wild goats who stand on their hind legs in order to reach them. This carving reminds one of the Gate of Mycenae, where two lionesses stand on their hind quarters on both sides of an altar or sacred object. The dress of the deity reminds one of the Minoan goddess Rhea.

Ivories belonging to the Nineteenth Dynasty were discovered at Megiddo which betray the Phoenician features, namely a blending of the art of the surrounding nations with Egyptian influence predominating. The ivories in question reveal Egyptian, Aegean, and Syrian influences. The tradition of ivory carving was maintained in Phoenicia during the country's Golden Age. The ivories of Samaria, (Pl. 5) Arslan Tash, and Nimroud betray the same technique. It is highly probably that Phoenician artists were commissioned in each case with execution of the carving and in some cases they probably had to go to the cities and do the carving on the spot.

In sculpture again, the Phoenicians copied the Egyptian style, but their figures are less stiff and more rounded. However, the execution is far inferior to that of Egypt. In the temple of the Lady of Byblos, three badly preserved colossal statues were discovered; one represents the Lady of Byblos seated on a throne, another seated figure which the excavator judges to be that of *El* the consort of *Baalat Gebal*; and the third figure, which is standing, is said to represent *Aliyan* or *Eshmun*. The colossi are heavy, their upper portions have disappeared, and age has played havoc on the calcareous limestone from which they were carved. One of the these is at present in the National Museum in Beirut. They are interesting but hardly appeal to our aesthetic sense. All belong to the Early Bronze Age.

Of the Middle Bronze Age, a fine stele was discovered at Ras Shamra by Schaeffer. It represents *Baal*, bearded and wearing a pointed headdress ornamented with two horns projecting forward (Pl. 4). His hair falls in long tresses over his shoulders; in his right hand he brandishes a mace, and in his left he holds a thunderbolt which is represented by a lance ending in leaflike branches. A dagger ending in a curved point is attached to his belt. Over an altar in front of him stands a small figure in the attitude of prayer. Below are representations of mountains.

From the Golden Age of Phoenicia we have a similar statue

from Amrit (Fig. 27, p.102). It represents *Baal* standing over the head and tail of a lion; the latter in turn stands over two mountains which are represented in the Babylonian style by a pile of discs. *Baal* wears an Egyptian crown of Upper Egypt, with feathers over the crown of the headdress and an uraeus at the front; his hair falls in tresses as far as his shoulder but does not drop below it. He wears a sleeveless close-fitting short tunic. In his right hand he brandishes a scimitar and in his left he holds a lion cub by its hind legs. Over his head is a crescent above which there is a winged disc.

In this stele we have a blending of various traits of ancient art, Babylonian, Egyptian, North Syrian, Cappadocian and Hurrite.

From Byblos comes a stele (of which there is a cast in the National Museum in Beirut) of great importance. According to the inscription on the stele it represents Yahumelek, king of Byblos, offering a sacrifice to the Lady of Byblos. The goddess is represented seated on a throne, dressed in the guise of Hathor, the Egyptian cow-goddess. She wears a long tight-fitting tunic of a light fabric. On her head, she wears a crown surmounted by a sun-disc between two horns. In her left hand she holds a staff ornamented at the top with a lotus flower, while the right arm is extended over the king of Byblos in the attitude of benediction. The king of Byblos is represented approaching the goddess; he is bearded and wears a cylindrical head-dress like a kalpak, with his long hair falling over his shoulders. In his right hand he holds a libation bowl, and the left arm is raised in salutation. The king wears a long tunic reaching to the ankles, and over it a short-sleeved mantle (Fig. 28, p. 109). The Lady of Byblos or Ashtart is entirely Egyptian in conception and execution, while Yahumelek himself is entirely Syrian. The stele belongs to the Persian Period. Examples can be multiplied of Phoenician art as expressed in sculpture but the above examples are sufficient to show the composite nature of the art, and the various influences which helped to mould it. Before closing our discussion of Phoenician sculpture we may in passing mention the stele at Ghineh, not far from Afqa, above Byblos. It represents Adonis being gored by a wild boar while close by Ashtart sits weeping ; it belongs to the Roman Period.

Ceramic Art

Let us now turn to the most important art, the ceramic art of the Phoenicians. The importance and value of the potter's art and its development was realized by all archaeologists [1] in the second half of the last century when archaeology advanced from being a hobby of the rich to be a science of great importance. In the absence of written records, archaeologists realized pottery was of prime importance in dating the various archaeological levels in any site, and thus made it possible to reconstruct its history. Briefly the importance of pottery may here be summarized as follows:

Pottery was discovered at an early stage in man's history, about 5000 B.C., and continued in use down to the present day; the forms and technique of making pottery changed from century to century, and sometimes even from generation to generation, so much so that pottery can be used as a criterion or yard-stick for dating occupation levels in historical sites where other objects fail the archaeologists.

Clay, from which pottery is made, is plentiful and always at hand, unlike metal, which requires laborious and expensive processes of mining and smelting. Hence pottery vessels are more plentiful, and their presence in historical sites is proportionately far greater than vessels in other materials such as stone, metal or glass.

Thirdly, pottery is more durable ; whereas metal vessels oxidize and disintegrate in the damp soil of Phoenicia, pottery vessels remain more or less intact. Even when broken, pottery vessels can be mended and restored to their original shape.

Fourthly, pottery-making is an artistic expression and it can be used as a yard-stick to measure the artistic taste of the people who made it. People with good taste generally produce graceful vases, whereas people lacking in good taste produce hideous forms.

Archaeologists, in their efforts to classify ancient pottery chronologically have used various criteria. Many books have been and are being written on the subject, which if put together would assume the size of a large encyclopaedia. Briefly, however, the criteria used in dating pottery may be summarized into ware, colour, method of making and firing, form and shape, the loci or places in the levels or strata of a site in which they were found, and proximity to dateable objects in their place of discovery.

With these criteria the following chronological scheme has been adopted for the pottery of Phoenicia:

[1] Starting with the late Sir Flinders Petrie.

Culture

Neolithic	5000-4000 B.C.
Chalcolithic	4000-3100 B.C.
Early Bronze	3100-2300 B.C.
Intermediate	2300-1900 B.C.
Middle Bronze	1900-1500 B.C.
Late Bronze	1500-1150 B.C.
Early Iron	1150-900 B.C.
Middle Iron	900-550 B.C.
Late Iron or Persian	550-330 B.C.
Hellenistic	330-64 B.C.
Roman	64 B.C.-A.D. 330
Byzantine	A.D. 330-636.

Neolithic pottery was discovered at both Byblos and Ras Shamra. It consists of hand-made vessels, under-fired, decorated with finger-nail or bone incisions, and provided with loop or ledge handles; the pottery is tempered with flint grits, as well as fragments of bone or straw (Pl. 8).

The Chalcolithic ceramic industry of the Near East showed a great improvement on that of the Neolithic Period. It is true that flint and limestone grits, sometimes larger than those of the previous period, continued to be used, but the pottery of the period went through various stages of decoration. At the beginning of the period, the pottery was generally painted in red or black geometric designs over a burnished surface. This type of pottery is known as Tell el Halaf ware after the place in North Syria where it was first discovered. Tell el Halaf pottery was followed by thin delicate pottery which was painted in black or brown with abstract designs over a greenish cream surface. It is called Tell el Ubeid ware by archaeologists as it was first discovered on a site of the same name near Ur in Lower Mesopotamia. The Tell el Ubeid ware after a long lease of life eventually gave place to unpainted grey pottery which was highly burnished and which was first discovered at Uruk in Lower Mesopotamia and thus came to be called by archaeologists as the Uruk ware. The Uruk ware was succeeded by the Jemdet Nasr pottery, which was made of thick ware and painted in polychrome designs. Examples of these four types with somewhat local modifications were discovered

71

at Ras Shamra but not at Byblos where only pottery related to the Urukian was discovered (Pl. 8).

The local pottery of these two early stages is entirely made by hand.

With the coming of the Early Bronze Age, the technique of firing greatly improved. The pots of this period resound with a metallic ring when tapped. The ware in this period is still gritty, but the grits are invariably of flint or chert, and although still numerous, they are much smaller in size than the grits employed in the preceding period. The pots of this period were decorated with a slip, and some of them were burnished with a pebble in a diamond pattern (Pl. 8). A highly burnished black or red ware and decorated with finger grooves makes its appearance about 2600 B.C. It is known as Khirbat el Kerak ware, after the place south of the Sea of Galilee where it was first discovered. The potter's wheel was invented towards the beginning of the Early Bronze Age, but some vessels continued to be handmade.

With the Middle Bronze Age, pottery reached its highest stage of perfection. The use of the wheel became universal, and new graceful forms made their appearance for the first time. There were for example juglets with piriform (pear-shaped) bodies and button bases (Pl. 8). In the early stages they were decorated with a red slip and were highly burnished. Towards the latter part of the period, a cream slip replaced the red slip and polychrome painting made its appearance. Also there were high bowls with trumpet shaped bases and carinated bodies (Pl. 8). The ware is very thin and crisp due to the use of the potter's wheel and the advanced technique in firing the pots. The forms of the pottery in this period are unequalled in grace until the Hellenistic Period. A special type of juglet with a piriform body, a button base, a short thin neck and a double strand handle, made of black ware and decorated with geometrical motifs with pin points and filled with white makes its appearance in the eighteenth century B.C. It is associated with the arrival of the Hyksos. The pottery is called the Tell el Yehudiyeh ware by archaeologists after the place in Egypt of the same name where it was first discovered by Petrie. Tell el Yehudiyeh is generally identified with Avaris, the capital of the Hyksos. The Middle Bronze Age was a period of great international trade. In consequence a number of Middle Minoan vases from Crete were found at Ras Shamra and

Byblos, and Egyptian pottery was found in great quantities at Byblos and elsewhere, while Phoenician pottery was discovered in several places in the Near East outside Phoenicia.

The Late Bronze Age is notable for the large variety of its pots. International trade which assumed such large proportions in the previous period made further spurts in this. Although there was little difference in pottery-making techniques locally, local pottery is not so well made (Pl. 9). However imported pots are very numerous. First Cypriote and later Mycenaean pottery came into Phoenicia in large numbers. Cypriote bowls with wish-bone handles, Cypriote *bilbils* or jugs made of thin crispy ware, with a slanting neck, painted brown in imitation of bronze (the so-called base ring ware) are ubiquitous. Later, Mycenaean pyxes, amphorae and stirrup vases with false spouts deluged the Near East (Pl. 9). At Ras Shamra Mycenaean pots were found literally by the thousand. In a small tomb at Sarepta, (modern Sarafend, about half way between Tyre and Sidon) out of about sixty vessels retrieved, only twenty were locally made, while the others were imported from Mycenae or from a Mycenaean pottery kiln in Cyprus. Mycenaean pottery is recognized by its buff colour, highly polished surface and monochrome painting either in brown or orange-red, but above all by its characteristic forms.

The Dorian Invasion of Greece in the twelfth century B.C. disrupted the Aegean world and with it the rest of the Near East as we have seen. The Aegeans who eventually settled in Phoenicia brought with them their pottery-making techniques, but of course the local clay being different, their pots assumed a slightly different appearance. We thus find in Phoenicia alone, and for a short time in Philistia, a continuation of the Mycenaean ceramic industry under new conditions. This is the reason why the pottery of the hinterland of Syria and Palestine is so different from that of Phoenicia and Philistia during the Early Iron Age, which saw the rise of Phoenicia as a great sea-power and ushered in her Golden Age. Whereas in the hinterland new forms start making their appearance, unrelated or only remotely related to the pottery of the preceding periods, in Phoenicia there is no break in the development of pottery styles or decoration. Sir Leonard Woolley has already drawn attention to the similarity between Cypro-Phoenician pottery of the Early Iron Age and Mycenaean pottery of the Late Bronze Age and to the great difference between the same pottery and the pottery of the hinterland. [1] He attributed the success of the Phoenician traders in Cyprus to the fact that both Cyprus and Phoenicia were at the time under Aegean domination, and to the blood relationship of the Cypriote Aegeans with their brethren in Phoenicia. In fact he goes on to say that it was the Aegeans who inherited the thalassocracy over the Western Mediterranean after 1200 B.C. but under a different name. Whereas the present writer agrees with the main purport of Sir Leonard Woolley's views he believes that the Semitic element in the population of Phoenicia played a greater role than Sir Leonard cared to concede them. It was not the Aegean lords of Phoenicia, but rather the nation or race resulting from the fusion of the two races, the Semitic-Canaanites or proto-Phoenicians and Aegeans which is responsible for the Cypro-Phoenician culture.

The pottery of the Early Iron Age of Phoenicia is generally decorated with parallel horizontal polychrome bands around the rim, the body and the base (Pl. 10). In addition the shoulder is often divided into panels or metopes by vertical bands, sometimes enclosing a diamond pattern, dropping from the band at the neck to the top band around the middle of the body. The forms include juglets with ring bases, globular bodies, and handles attached one end at the middle of the neck and the other at the shoulder. Some jugs are provided with a long open spout and a strainer (Pl. 10). These it has been suggested are beer drinking jugs, and the strainer was intended to stop the husks from choking the drinker. [2] In the Middle Iron Age, the horizontal bands give place to concentric circles which kept increasing with time so that by about the sixth century B.C. they were so numerous as to become nauseating. In addition to the flat ring based juglets, juglets with semi round bases were introduced which with time became barrel-shaped.

There were also craters and pilgrim bottles, which were an adaptation of earlier forms. They are distinguished by their polychrome decoration and in the case of pilgrim bottles, by their more globular form, as against the lentoid form of the Late Bronze Age.

[1] Cf. *Syria*, Vol. II, pp. 177-194.
[2] Cf. Albright: *Archaeology of Palestine*, p. 115.

By the middle of the sixth century B.C., Attic pots started making their appearance both in Cyprus and in Phoenicia. Gradually, Phoenician and Cypriote ceramic art proceeded to part company and follow independent lines of development. Phoenicia severed its cultural relations with Cyprus on account of the rising power of Persia in the Near East and the country became more influenced by the ceramic industry of the hinterland. This state of affairs persisted until the last quarter of the fourth century B.C., when Alexander, in his march of victory, brought with him artisans and craftsmen who introduced Hellenistic techniques in pottery making and introduced the slender forms which were prevalent in the Greek world. The local potters eagerly copied the Greek models and the culture became Hellenistic. Slender elliptical forms took the place of globular forms. Under the Romans, Arretine pottery, which has a lustrous glazed red ware, was introduced into the country and locally copied. The rise of the Roman Empire was accompanied by a uniformity of culture which embraced the ceramic industry. Pottery forms were made on the same pattern in Sidon, Corinth and Gaul. Horizontal ribbing was introduced in the first century A.D., first on cooking pots; but gradually it replaced all other form of decoration. Ribbing was at first fine and shallow; but in process of time the ribs became coarse and deep, and finally during the Byzantine Period they degenerated into deep heavy ribs, lost their curved outline and became square in section.

Glass

Faience or glazed paste was in common use during the Eighteenth and Nineteenth Dynasties in Egypt. In the levels corresponding with this period, many faience beads, amulets, figurines and vessels, made in Egypt, were discovered at Megiddo, Beisan (Beth Shan), Tell ed-Duwair (Lachish) and elsewhere. In Byblos similar beads were discovered, some no doubt of Egyptian origin, and others locally manufactured. Faience of the Eighteenth Dynasty is more gritty than that of the Nineteenth Dynasty, which approached glass in texture. However real glass was unknown until the twelfth century. The earliest glass vessels were made in Phoenicia. They were made of moulded glass often consisting of strands of various colours (Pl. 10). The glass is translucent. Sometimes it was decorated with animal or geometrical motifs in glass paste which were applied on the vessel.

75

It was not till the first century that a Sidonian invented glass blowing, and glass became transparent.

Phoenician glass was famous in antiquity; but its methods of production were complicated, and it remained a luxury which only the rich could afford. However with the invention of blown glass, the industry received a new fillip and glass vessels were mass produced. Thus, whereas in some of the tombs earlier than

FIGURE 1

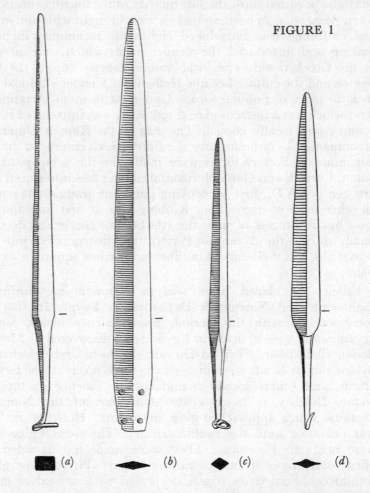

Bronze daggers (a) (b) Amorite, c. 2,200 B.C. (c) (d) Late Bronze Age, 1,600-1,200 B.C.

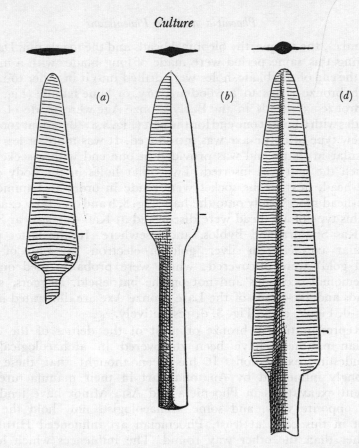

FIGURE 2 *Bronze spear-heads* (a) *Middle Bronze Age* (b) (c) *Late Bronze Age*

the first century a glass vessel or two were sometimes discovered, in the tombs of the first century they were generally discovered by the dozen.

Metal objects

In metallurgy, the Phoenicians at the outset copied Egypt for their common weapons and tools, but for their figurines, although influenced by Egypt they developed an art of their own. From about 3000 to 2300 B.C., their tools were restricted to axe-heads (Fig. 3, a) and daggers, which were made of heavy metal. With the arrival of the torque wearers sometime in the twenty first century B.C. several new types made their appearance including the socketed spear head (Fig. 2, b), the socketed battle-axe (Fig. 3, b and c), the torque, the biconical beads and the toggle pin. Daggers during this same period were made of long blades with a midrib. At the end of the blade, holes were drilled into it in order to rivet it with bronze rivets to a wooden, ivory, or bone handle (Fig. 1, b).

Bronze axe-heads in the Early Bronze Age were made of metal blades with a hole at one end for the haft (Fig. 3,a). By about 2000B.C. a new type of battle-axe was introduced. It was more or less semi-circular in shape and was provided at one end with a socket into which the haft was inserted. Two other holes in the body of the axe-head, next to the socket were made in order to hammer the axe-head more firmly onto the haft (Fig. 3, b and c). Many examples of this type of axe-head were discovered at Kafr-Jarra, near Sidon, at Ras Shamra and Byblos, and elsewhere. In the latter place, similar axe-heads in silver, gold or electron (an alloy of silver and gold) were discovered, which were probably used only on ceremonial occasions and not on the battlefield. Daggers, spear-heads and axe-heads of the Late Bronze Axe are illustrated in Fig. 1, c-d, Fig. 2, c and Fig. 3, d, respectively.

Representation in bronze of most of the deities of the Phoe-nician pantheon have been discovered in archaeological and clandestine excavations. It has been thought that these were strongly influenced by Anatolian art in their manufacture. But recent excavations in Phoenicia and Asia Minor have tended to the opposite view, and some archaeologists now hold the view that in this case, at least, Phoenician art influenced Hittite art rather than the other way round. The influences which helped to mould Phoenician representational art are a combination of Egyptian, Mesopotamian, Anatolian and Aegean influences.

Amongst the various figurines discovered in Phoenicia, men-tion may be made of Ashtart in her role as goddess of fertility (Pl. 7) and of Reshef-Baal in his role as a god of thunder, rain, storm and war (Pl. 6). The earlier figurines are flat, being moulded of thin metal with no attempt at perspective and less attempt at reproducing the correct anatomical details; the head was made unduly large; the neck was too long or entirely missing; the arms and legs sprang from about the same place; the trunk was absent and the breasts, when present, were placed immediately above the thighs. The features are lifeless and appear incom-plete and skeletal. However by the middle of the Second Mil-

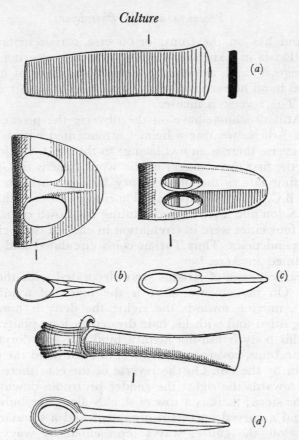

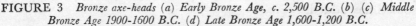

FIGURE 3 *Bronze axe-heads* (a) *Early Bronze Age, c. 2,500 B.C.* (b) (c) *Middle Bronze Age 1900-1600 B.C.* (d) *Late Bronze Age 1,600-1,200 B.C.*

lennium more attention was paid to anatomy; the arms, legs and torso were rounded and were more realistic. Some figurines were covered with gold leaf (Pl. 7). Ashtart is easily recognized by her prominent sexual organs, while Reshef can be recognized by his high conical hat, his short tunic and the thunderbolt he wields in his right hand (Pl. 6).

Numismatic Art

The earliest coins to be used in Phoenicia were the Persian gold darics and silver sigloi; and the Attic drachma, which was introduced into the country through Athenian trade. Athenian trade was at its height in the fifth century B.C. The daric is oval in shape and has on the front, or obverse, a representation of the king of Persia in a kneeling-running position, wearing the *kidaris* and *kandys*, [1] and drawing a bow with his right hand, while in his left hand he carries a spear, and on his shoulder a quiver of arrows. The reverse is incuse.

The Attic drachmae have on the obverse the profile of a head of Pallas Athena wearing a helmet ornamented with olive sprays; on the reverse there is an owl facing; to the right, written from the top, are the first three letters of the word Athens in Greek : ΑΘΕ.

Sometime late in the fifth century B.C. or early in the fourth century B.C. the most important Phoenician cities such as Aradus, Byblos, Sidon and Tyre started minting their own coins. The coins of these four cities were in circulation in each of these cities and in their dependencies. Thus Tyrian coins circulated and some even were minted in Acre. [2]

The earliest coins of Aradus were decorated with the following devices: On the obverse there is the figure of a marine deity (Dagon), moving towards the right; the deity is human to the waist, bearded and with his hair dressed in long plaits; the lower part of his body is fish-like with a bifid tail and dorsal, pectoral and ventral fins, covered with scales; in each hand the deity holds a dolphin by the tail. On the reverse of the coin there is a galley moving towards the right; the rudder protrudes downwards from below the stern; there is a row of shields along the bulwark of the galley and a curved uncertain ornament and a standard over the poop; below the galley, waves represented by wavy lines, are sometimes added.

FIGURE 4   *Coin of Aradus, Persian Period*

Soon afterwards, we do not know quite when, Dagon was

---

[1]   The kidaris is a cylindrical headdress, and the kandys are the wide trousers reaching to the ankle where they are gathered.

[2]   Cf. Quarterly of the Department of Antiquities in Palestine, Vol. I, p. 10.

replaced by the head of a male deity, possibly Baal Yam ("Lord of the Sea") the equivalent of the Greek Poseidon or Roman Neptune, who wears a pointed beard represented by lines, while his hair and whiskers are represented by pellets. On the reverse below the waves, a hippocamp, or a dolphin is sometimes added, while above the galley, the Phoenician letters MA standing for Melek Arwad (King of Aradus) sometimes appear (Fig. 4).

These coins continued in circulation until Alexander captured Aradus in 333 B.C. when a new mint was established by Alexander, at which coins of Alexander were struck with the monogram of Aradus Ｒ.

FIGURE 5   *Coin of Byblos, Persian Period*

The coins of Byblos, which were first struck early in the fourth century B.C. bear the following devices: On the obverse there is a galley sailing towards the left; along the bulwark of the galley there are three hoplites wearing crested helmets and carrying round shields; below the galley there is a hippocamp (sea horse). On the reverse the earliest coins have a vulture standing towards the left, over the body of a ram which is lying on the ground. In later coins, the vulture is replaced by a lion which stands towards the left over the body of a bull. Later still, the lion is represented bringing down the bull, while on the obverse, in addition to the usual design waves are represented by wavy lines between the galley and the hippocamp, and below the hippocamp, there is a murex shell. The later coins are inscribed in the margin on the reverse with the name of the king of Byblos during whose reign they were struck. The king may be either Elpaal, Azbaal, Ainel or Adramelek (Fig. 5).

The earliest coins of Sidon, struck towards the end of the fifth century B.C. (possibly by Eshmunazar) carry the following

81

devices: On the obverse, there is a war-galley sailing towards the left with the sail furled, and with two ropes hanging on either side of it; the mast of the galley is supported by two stays; a double rudder may sometimes be added under the square stern; a row of shields appears along the bulwark; there is an uncertain curved ornament over the poop, together with a standard surmounted by a globe and crescent; below the galley there are waves represented by two zigzag lines. On the reverse, the king of Persia is seated in a chariot drawn by three horses racing towards the left; the chariot is driven by a charioteer who leans forward and holds the reins of the horse nearest to him with his left hand; the king of Persia wears the *kidaris* and *kandys* and raises his right hand upwards.

FIGURE 6   *Coin of Sidon, Persian Period*

In later coins, struck early in the fourth century B.C. there is added to the obverse a battlemented fortress representing the city walls of Sidon, with five turreted towers behind the galley. Later still about 384-370 B.C. a new variety of coins appears which was probably struck by Bodashtart, who rebuilt the temple of Eshmun at Sidon. On the obverse a war-galley with oars is represented sailing towards the left; along the bulwarks there is a row of shields; at the prow there is a small armed figure placed as a figure-head while at the stern there is a curved ornament supporting a globe-and-crescent standard as before. The fortress disappears and its place is taken by the Phoenician letter B for Bodashtart. The reverse is similar to the coins previously described except that in addition, a figure wearing the crown of Upper Egypt (possibly representing the king of Sidon) and holding a sceptre in his right hand decorated with an animal's head, walks behind the chariot (Fig. 6).

The coins of 370-358 B.C. are similar to this except that the initials of the king's name appear in some cases on the obverse and in others on the reverse. Thus on the coins of Straton I (Abdashtart in Phoenician) the letters AB in Phoenician characters appear above the chariot on the reverse. The coins of Tennes, Tabnit in Phoenician, (354-348 B.C.) have the letters TA above the chariot. Similarly the coins of Evagoras (348-342 B.C.) bear the Phoenician letters OO ('Ain 'Ain), the coins of Straton II (Abdashtart 342-333 B.C.) the Phoenician letters AB, and the satrap Mazaeus the Phoenician letters MZ over the chariot.

FIGURE 7   *Coin of Tyre, Persian Period*

The earliest coins of Tyre, struck between 450 and 400 B.C. are decorated with the following designs: On the obverse, there is a dolphin swimming towards the right over waves represented by three wavy bands; below the dolphin there is a murex shell. On the reverse, there is an owl standing with its head facing straight; it carries a crook and flail over its shoulder. This design was no doubt inspired by Athenian coins. Later, between 400 and 332 B.C. the reverse does not change except for the addition of numerals, but on the obverse, Melqarth-Herakles, the patron deity of Tyre, appears wearing a beard and riding on a hippocamp with curled wings, swimming towards the right; Melqarth holds the reins of the hippocamp in his right hand and in his left he holds a strung bow; two lines of waves are represented below the hippocamp, and a dolphin appears swimming towards the right under the waves (Fig. 7).

The dies of all these coins are the work of Phoenicians, and perhaps in them we see Phoenician pictorial art of the fifth and fourth centuries B.C. at its best.

During the reign of Alexander, of Philip Arridaeus and of Alexander Aegos, the usual type of Alexandrine coin was struck in these four cities; on the obverse, a profile of the head of Herakles appears looking right and wearing the lion's skin; on the reverse, Zeus seated on his throne facing left, weaing a *himation*, [1] holding an eagle in his outstretched right hand and resting with his left hand on his sceptre. Behind the throne in the right field is the name of Alexander or Philip. In front of Zeus, in other words in the field on the left, there is either a monogram or a symbol of the city in which the coin was struck. In the case of Aradus the monogram is Я or the Greek letters AR, of Byblos B,[2] of Sidon ΣI and of Tyre 𐤕 or the three Greek letters TYR. In addition some coins struck at Tyre carry the club as a symbol. The dies, whether made in Greece or in Phoenicia by Greek engravers, are Hellenistic and cannot be strictly speaking called Phoenician.

During the Golden Age of Hellenism, Phoenicia was held at first by the Ptolemies of Egypt, and later by the Seleucid kings of Antioch. After the Battle of Ipsus (301 B.C.) Ptolemaic coins were in circulation in Phoenicia, but after the battle of Paneion in 200 B.C. they were replaced by Seleucid coins. Ptolemaic silver coins generally bear on the obverse the head of king Ptolemy I Soter in profile facing right, wearing a diadem, and on the reverse an eagle standing facing left. Around along the margin of the coin is the legend "King Ptolemy" in Greek (BASILEOS PTOLE-MAIOY). Seleucid coins generally have on the obverse the head of the reigning Seleucid king in profile facing right and wearing a diadem, and on the reverse, a nude figure of Apollo seated on the omphalos, with drapery over his waist. In his right hand Apollo holds an arrow and with his left he rests on a bow. The name of the reigning king is written in the left field in front of Apollo, while behind him is the Greek word for king, BASILEOS. [3]

Even before the disruption of the Seleucid Kingdom in 129 B.C. Aradus and Berytus regained their autonomy and the right to mint their own coins. Aradus acquired the right in 259 B.C. and Berytus in 197 B.C. They were followed by Tyre in 126 B.C., by Tripolis in 112 B.C., by Sidon in 110 B.C. and by Byblos in 83 B.C.

[1] A winding sheet.
[2] It is not certain whether these coins were struck at Byblos or Beirut.
[3] These are the commoner Seleucid coins, but there are other varieties.

In the first century B.C practically every Phoenician city became autonomous if not independent and minted its own coins. This state of affairs continued until 64 B.C. when Pompey the Great captured Syria and converted it into a Roman Province. The chief Phoenician cities were allowed, true to Roman policy of partiality to cities, to retain a certain measure of autonomy and to mint their own coins.

It would be far beyond the scope of this book to give a detailed description of the coins of Phoenicia from the second century B.C. to the end of the Roman Period. However some general remarks on the more notable coins of the cities of Phoenicia may not be out of place, and may help the reader to identify them when the occasion arises.

ARADUS Between 260 and 174 B.C.

obverse: *Head of Zeus, facing right bearded and laureate.*

reverse : *Prow of galley sailing toward the left, with Athena fighting as figurehead. Above prow : monogram AP.*

FIGURE 8   *Coin of Aradus, Seleucid Period*

obverse: *Bust of Tyche wearing a turreted crown and necklace, carrying a palm branch over her shoulder.*

reverse : *Poseidon nude to the waist, seated on the prow of a galley, holding a wreath in extended right hand (Figure 8)*

FIGURE 9   *Coin of Aradus, Seleucid period*

Between 174 and 110 B.C.

obverse: *Bee with outstretched wings.*

reverse : *Stag standing towards the right in front of a palm tree. Name of city in Greek letters on the right (Figure 9)*

FIGURE 10   *Coin of Aradus, Seleucid Period*

Between 137 and 46 B.C.

obverse: *Bust of Tyche (City-goddess) facing right, wearing a turreted crown and veil.*

reverse : *Nike (Victory), winged, advancing towards the left, wearing a long tunic, girt at the waist, and holding an aphlaston in her right hand and a palm branch in her left. The name of the city in Greek letters behind Nike (Figure 10)*

FIGURE 11   *Coin of Berytus, Seleucid Period*

BERYTUS Second Century B.C.

obverse: *Bust of Tyche facing right wearing a turreted crown and carrying a palm branch over her shoulder.*

reverse : *Baal-Berit (lord of Beirut) wearing a low kalathos (cylindrical headdress) and himation over the lower part of his body and over shoulder, standing in a car draw by four hippocamps; he holds a phial in his right hand and a trident in his left. There is a Phoenician inscription on the left, and on the right the Greek letters for Berytion (Figure 11)*

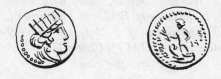

FIGURE 12   *Coin of Berytus, Seleucid Period*

Second type:

obverse: *Same as former type.*

reverse : *Ashtart wearing a long tunic standing on the prow of a galley ; she holds an aphlaston in her right hand, and rests her left hand on her hip. Name of Beirut is on the left in Phoenician and there is Greek monogram on the right (Figure 12)*

FIGURE 13   *Coin of Berytus, Seleucid Period*

Third type: First Century B.C.

obverse: *Same as former type,*

reverse : *A dolphin entwined around an upright trident between the caps of the Dioscuri (the Twins). In the field* BHPYTIΩN *in Greek (Figure 13)*

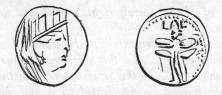

FIGURE 14   *Coin of Byblos, Seleucid Period*

BYBLOS First Century B.C.

obverse: *Bust of Tyche facing right, wearing a turreted crown and veil.*

reverse : *Kronos standing, facing, nude, with three pairs of wings. Above, is the name of Byblos in Phoenician LGBL, in the right field the monogram of Byblos, and below the name of Kronos in Phoenician : Q DMT (Figure 14)*

MARATHUS Between 227 and 225 B.C.

obverse: *Head of Tyche facing right, wearing turreted crown,*

reverse : *Marathus, patron deity and legendary founder of Marathus seated on a pile of circular shields, nude except for drapery over the waist. In the right field downwards appears the name of Marathus in Greek and on the left the date in Phoenician numerals.*

FIGURE 15   *Coin of Marathus, Seleucid Period*

obverse: *Head of Berenice veiled.*

reverse : *Marathos, founder of the city, draped above the middle, holding aphlaston and resting elbow on column (Figure 15)*

SIDON 2nd Century B.C.

obverse: *Bust of Tyche facing right, draped and wearing a turreted crown.*

reverse : *Rudder placed horizontally. Above and below Phoenician inscription meaning "To the Sidonians, mother of Camb, Apha Kat and Tyre". To this reverse there is another common variant namely Europa facing, seated on a bull, holding an inflated veil.*

FIGURE 16   *Coin of Sidon, Seleucid Period*

Period of Autonomy: 109 BC.-AD. 44.

obverse: *Same as other types.*

reverse : *Eagle facing left, with right claw resting on the prow of a galley, and carrying a palm branch over the right shoulder. In the field the name of Sidon in Greek and date in Greek letters (Figure 16)*

FIGURE 17   *Coin of Tripoli, Seleucid Period*

TRIPOLI 2nd-1st Century BC.

obverse: *Busts of the Dioscuri (Gemini or Heavenly Twins) joined together and facing right; both busts are draped, and there is a star above each.*

reverse : *Tyche standing, facing left, wearing a turreted crown, long tunic and mantle. She holds the horn of abundance (cornucopia) in her left hand and rests with her right hand on the tiller of a rudder. The name of Tripoli in Greek is written in the right field (Figure 17)*

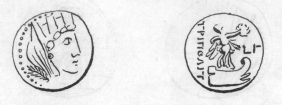

FIGURE 18   *Coin of Tripoli, Seleucid Period*

obverse: *Head of Tyche wearing turreted crown and veil, holding palm branch over shoulder.*

reverse : *Nike standing right on prow of a galley, holding wreath in left hand. Name in Greek on left side, date in right field (Figure 18)*

FIGURE 19   *Coin of Tyre, Seleucid Period*

TYRE Period of Autonomy:126 B.C. — 66. A.D.
Silver.

obverse: *Bust of Melqarth-Herakles facing right, with slight whisker, wearing a laurel wreath over his head and a lion-skin knotted around his neck.*

reverse : *Eagle standing, facing left, with its right claw on the beak of a ship and carrying a palm branch over its right shoulder. Name of Tyre and date in Greek letters in the margin around (Figure 19)*

FIGURE 20   *Coin of Tyre, Seleucid Period*

observe: *Head of Melqarth facing right, wearing laurel wreath.*

reverse : *Eagle standing towards the left holding a palm branch. In left field club of Heracles, around, the name in Greek. To this reverse, there were several variants which include a galley, or club (the club of Herakles) in the place of the palm tree (Figure 20)*

The coins which have just been described are only a selection of the most important coins of Phoenicia. If the interest of the reader has been aroused to such an extent as to require more information, he is advised to consult some of the books listed in the Bibliography at the end of the book.

When Phoenicia, together with Syria, was converted into a Roman Province, the various autonomous Phoenician cities were allowed to mint their own coins. Phoenician city coins struck during the Roman Empire generally bear the bust of the emperor, in most cases wearing a laurel wreath around his head, with his name and titles around the margin in Latin or Greek. On the reverse of each coin, there is generally represented a feature of the minting city, the name of the city and sometimes the date. It would be sufficient here to give a list of the most important of these reverses.

FIGURE 21   *Coin of Aradus, Roman Period*

ARADUS

Humped bull galloping towards the right (Figure 21)
Tall vase and two palm branches, one on either side
Tyche seated on a rudder, nude to the waist, and holding a cornucopia
  containing a bunch of grapes
A cypress tree with a lion on the left and a bull on the right confronted
Temple of Tyche

FIGURE 22   *Coin of Berytus, Roman Period*

BERYTUS

Prow of galley
A curved hook (lituus)
Dolphin entwined round trident
Two legionary eagles between two standards
Founder of city ploughing with an ox and a cow (Figure 22)
Poseidon, nude, standing facing left, with his foot on the prow of a galley,
  holding a dolphin head downwards
Temple of Ashtart
Dionysos, holding wine-skin
Ashtart as city-goddess

FIGURE 23   *Coin of Byblos, Roman Period*

BYBLOS

Kronos, nude, with six wings
Isis wearing a crown, long tunic and mantle flying behind her, standing
*   facing left, on a raft*
Temple of Ashtart (Figure 23)

FIGURE 24   *Coin of Sidon, Roman Period*

SIDON

Europa seated on a bull galloping towards the right (Figure 24)
Car of Ashtart (Figure 25)
Kadmos running towards the left, wearing a cloak fastened around the
*   neck and pointing forward with his right arm*
Ashtart, standing on the prow of a galley, carrying a cruciform standard
Temple of Ashtart
Dido
Three military standards
Agonistic Table
The Ship Argo
Dionysos carrying wine-skin
Signs of the Zodiac
Eshmun wearing high boots

FIGURE 25 *Coin of Sidon, Roman Period*

TRIPOLI

The Dioscuri, nude both standing facing left, each resting with his left
*   hand on a spear and holding a phial in his right hand over his cap*
*   which is placed on the ground*
The caps of the Dioscuri each surmounted by a star

93

(Tripoli, continued)

The busts of the Dioscuri joined together facing right, and wearing laureate caps surmounted by stars

Ashtart standing on the prow of a galley holding a cruciform standard

Nike standing, facing left, on a galley holding a wreath in her right hand and palm branch in her left hand over her shoulder

Ashtart and the Dioscuri

Temple of Zeus

Galley with square sail moving towards the left

FIGURE 26   *Coin of Tyre, Roman Period*

TYRE

Founder of city as a ploughman, ploughing towards the right with a yoke of an ox and a cow; a legionary standard in the background

Ashtart, as city-goddess standing on the prow of a galley, crowned by a small Nike (victory)

Male figure sacrificing on an altar

Bull walking towards the right. (Figure 26)

Harpocrates, wearing a lotus flower over his head

Nike (victory) leaning against a column

Temple seen in perspective

Agonistic table on which are two prize crowns

Eagle standing facing with outstretched wings

Galley with oars and rudder sailing towards the right

Palm tree with two bunches of fruit

Temple of Ashtart

Dionysos nude, carrying wine-skin

Dido building Carthage

> *Kadmos in galley*
> *Quadriga*
> *Baetyl oval in shape*
> *Prize crown*
> *Melqarth-Herakles sacrificing*
> *Two baetyls*
> *Athena wearing crested helmet, tunic and mantle, seated on a throne*

In addition the provincial coins of Syria, struck at Antioch, circulated in Phoenicia. On the obverse they have the usual bust of the emperor with his name, title and attributes around the margin. On the reverse there is an eagle with outstretched wings. In the margin there is an abbreviated inscription in Greek signifying that they were struck by virtue of a senatorial decree and in the field the letters SC appear which are short for SENATUS CONSULTUM signifying the same thing.

Funerary Art

During the Neolithic Age, the inhabitants of Phoenicia, judging by the results of the excavations of Byblos buried their dead in "cradle" graves, that is within a circular or an oval row of upright stones. The dead were placed in a contracted position with the knee placed against the chin. During the Chalcolithic Period, jar burial was introduced. Large jars, generally provided with four handles were made for this purpose. Before firing, and when the jar was still leather hard by drying in the sun, a section, sufficiently large to make it possible to insert the body in it, was sliced from the side of the jar. The two sections of the jar were then fired. The dead body was introduced into the jar together with bowls of food and cruses containing drinks for sustenance in the after-life. In both the Neolithic and the Chalcolithic Periods, the dead were buried under the floors of the houses for two reasons. The first was sentimental: the relatives of the deceased wanted the departed to remain close to them; the second reason was more prosaic: the bereaved families of the time did not possess the necessary tools which would enable them to dig deep graves in the ground outside their houses, and beyond the reach of wild beasts. Under the floors of the houses the dead would be safe from the ravages of wild animals. It seems that people believed in those days that a dismembered body would not live in the after-life, or if he did, he would be living in torture and agony because of the dismemberment of his dead body.

From the Early Bronze Age down to the Late Bronze Age the dead were generally buried in small caves, either natural or artificially excavated in the rock outside the city-walls. Together with the body, jars were placed in the tombs no doubt containing liquids, as well as small dippers with which to draw the liquid from the jars, and bowls containing food. The personal belongings of the deceased, as well as his arms were also interred in the tomb, as it was thought that the dead person would require them in his after-life; the articles interred were generally those that were used by the deceased during his life-time such as weapons and tools, articles of furniture such as chairs and stools, personal ornaments and so on. It is sometimes possible to gauge the vocation or calling of the deceased from his funerary equipment. At Byblos, the royal cemetery was within the city-walls at the north-west corner of the city, but this was an exception, and out of deference to royalty. The tombs of the royal cemetery consisted of shafts about six or seven metres deep, which were sunk in the solid rock. At the bottom of the shaft chambers were excavated in the side of the rock, one chamber for each burial. The bodies were laid in limestone or basalt sarcophagi or coffins with bevelled edges. The sarcophagus, after the body had been laid in it, was covered by a massive stone lid, which so fitted over the bevelled edge of the sarcophagus that it was difficult to open without actually smashing it. Each lid was provided with four supports, two at each end which projected beyond both ends, or which were cut out of the top of the lid. Ropes were attached to the handles and thus the lid was slowly lowered into the Hypogeum. The funerary equipment of the various royal tombs discovered has already been described. Most of the sarcophagi are still at Byblos, but one, the sarcophagus of Ahiram, has been removed to the Beirut National Museum.

At Ras Shamra, several tombs were discovered belonging to the Late Bronze Age. They consisted of rooms built under the dwelling houses. Steps led straight down into the tomb which generally had a gabled roof, built by corbels or cantilevered stones in the style of the Mycenaean tombs. The funerary equipment followed the pattern adopted elsewhere and included a large number of pots of various sizes, and personal ornaments and accoutrements.

During the Iron Age, the Phoenicians buried their dead in chambers cut in the rock. Some of these may still be seen in the vicinity of Tyre and in the rock face between Tyre and Sidon. They generally consisted of a square ante-chamber cut in the rock, giving access to other burial chambers on three sides of it. The entrance to the chamber is generally a narrow low door, which was sealed with a block of stone after use. The funerary equipment varied from previous periods only in the changed pottery forms and the addition of glass vases, otherwise it was similar. The status of the deceased and his affluence during his lifetime can generally be gauged by the wealth or paucity of his funerary equipment.

During the Persian Period the architectural style of the tomb did not change much from the earlier periods. In addition to the usual locally manufactured pots and personal belongings met in earlier burials, it becomes now possible to find a few coins in the tomb such as Attic drachmae, gold *daries* and silver *sigloi* as well as local coins and Greek Attic vases. A Phoenician cemetery of this period was discovered at Athlit in Palestine. At Sidon a royal cemetery was discovered, just east of the city. It contained burials going back to the Persian Period and is an eloquent testimony of the composite nature of Phoenician art. Some of the sarcophagi are modelled on those of Egypt like the sarcophagus of Tabnit, now at Constantinople, and that of Eshmunazar, now in the Louvre Museum. Others betray Greek influence, like the anthropomorphic sarcophagi of which twenty six turned up at Sidon. The famous so-called sarcophagus of Alexander, the sarcophagi of the Satrap, the Lycian and the Weepers, are masterpieces of their kind. The four sarcophagi were discovered in the royal cemetery near Sidon, and were taken to Constantinople, as Phoenicia at the time of the discovery was part of the Ottoman Empire.

The sarcophagus of Alexander, the finest of the four, is made of Pentelic marble, especially imported from Attica in Greece for the purpose; it is lavishly and tastefully decorated in the Hellenistic style. On one of the long sides, there is carved a scene from the famous Battle of Issus in 333 B.C. Alexander can be readily recognized in the scene wearing the lion's skin surmounted by the Macedonian sign of royalty, a diadem or fillet of gold. The execution is of a very high order and the scene is alive with motion and the grim realism of a battle in earnest. The other long side is carved with a lion and gazelle hunt in which Alexander took part. Alexander appears about to strike a huge lion which was biting the chest of the horse of one of Alexander's knights. One of the ends of the sarcophagus is carved with a panther hunt, while the other together with the gables on either side of the lid depict further scenes from the Battle of Issus. The carving was made more vivid by painting of which traces still remain in parts. All the scenes are alive with movement, while the proportions, the setting and the space are so used as to make the sculpture perfect. The sarcophagus was, according to the consensus of opinion of historians and archaeologists, not made for Alexander, but its exquisite sculpture makes it a worthy resting place for the great conqueror.

The sarcophagus of the Weepers is also made of Pentelic marble. The sides of the lid are carved with *quadrigas* and knights on horseback moving at a slow pace as though in a funeral, while the sides of the sarcophagus itself represent the sides of an Ionic temple. Between each pair of columns stands a draped woman weeping, or with a dejected and sad expression on her face, mourning for the deceased. Below on the sides of the stylobate of the temple hunting scenes are represented on a much smaller scale.

The sarcophagi of the Lycian and the Satrap are both of Parian marble, brought from the Island of Paros in the Aegean. The lid of the first is cut like a lofty vault, and its height is about the same as that of the sarcophagus. Each end of the lid is carved with two sphinxes, sitting back to back on both sides of a small pillar. The long sides of the sarcophagus are carved with scenes from a boar hunt while each of the ends is decorated with a pair of fighting centaurs in high relief.

The sarcophagus of the Satrap is of similar form. It is decorated in relief on one of the long sides with the representation of a satrap or Persian provincial governor seated on a throne watching his servants examining a horse and a chariot; the other long side represents a scene from a panther hunt; it is very lively with motion and aptly reflects the excitement of the scene. On one of the two ends, the satrap is represented lying on a couch and partaking of a feast, while the other end represents four soldiers in lively conversation.

By an irony of fate these great works of Greek and Hellenistic sculpture were discovered in Phoenicia a few decades before the export of antiquities from Lebanon was controlled. Instead of gracing the National Museum in Beirut, where they rightly belong, they now form some of the most important treasures in the Museum of Istanbul, where a special wing was built to house them at the time of discovery.

During the Hellenistic Period the fashion of building mausolea over tombs came into fashion. The tombs in this period consisted of a *dromos* or passage cut in the rock, which led into an ante-chamber. Long narrow *loculi* were excavated in the side of the chamber for interring the bodies. Each *loculus* was then sealed effectively by a stone. Those who could afford it, built a monument above ground over the subterranean burial chamber. The monuments may be in the form of a pyramid resting on a high square base, or the tomb may be surmounted by a thimble-like structure over a high square base protected by four lions at the corners. Examples of both types of mausolea may be seen at Amrit (ancient Marathus). The Phoenicians during the Hellenistic Period also buried their dead in highly ornamented marble sarcophagi.

During the Roman Period the rich buried their dead in marble sarcophagi, but the ornamentation is simple and the execution is mediocre. However, a limestone sarcophagus was discovered at Sidon, which is decorated at one end in relief with the representation of a Phoenician galley, carved in relief with the sail unfurled. Sometime during the Roman Period, lead sarcophagi, embossed with garlands, cupids and other Classical motifs, were introduced. The improvident and the poor buried their dead either in clay coffins or in wooden coffins placed in loculi after the style of the Hellenistic Period. During the Byzantine Period, marble and lead sarcophagi continued to be used by the well-to-do, but the bulk of the population buried their dead in rectangular shafts cut in the rock, with two other graves cut along either side of the middle shaft to make the tomb capable of holding three bodies. Examples of these may be seen near Adlun.

The antiquities that one generally sees in Museums come mainly from tombs, as in tombs, the objects, whether glass, pottery or other fragile material were not subjected to such violent handling and rough treatment as objects discovered in occupation levels, hence they remained well preserved. In stratified levels, however, fragile vessels are almost invariably found broken and have to be mended if most of the fragments are retrieved.

Architecture

During the Neolithic Period the inhabitants of Phoenicia lived in rectangular or square huts built of lumps of mud tempered with straw over a stone foundation. The floors of these huts were paved with limestone crushed to powder and made into a paste, which after being laid, was beaten to form a hard concrete mass and polished. Examples of these may still be seen in some of the Neolithic huts at Byblos.

The roofs of these huts were built of branches of trees, leaves and mud. As their tree-felling instruments were inefficient, they could not cut large logs to span large rooms but could only lop off short branches; so they had to be content with constructing long narrow rooms.

During the Chalcolithic Period, the inhabitants of Phoenicia developed a new type of architecture which enabled them to build larger rooms. The plan of a Chalcolithic house is generally semi-circular or apsidal, very much like a modern horse-shoe. It was built of rectangular bricks made in moulds and it was roofed with animal skins placed over wooden rafters which rested at one end on a pole set up in the middle of the room, and at the other on the walls of the room. A Chalcolithic house in fact looked very much like a modern bell-tent of the Egyptian variety.

With the coming of the Early Bronze Age, and the availability of bronze implements both for felling large trees and for quarrying stone, the architecture of the period underwent great improvements. Hitherto, the early inhabitants of Phoenicia had to rely for their masonry, entirely on the loose stones that they could collect. Quarrying was unknown. From now on it was possible to quarry whatever stone was needed. As a result, large houses, consisting of several spacious square or rectangular rooms, came into being. The foundations and sometimes the entire ground floor were built of quarried roughly squared stones, and the gaps in the masonry were filled with stone chippings. The walls were then plastered inside and outside. The roof was built of large logs, either laid flat from the top of one wall to the other, or if the room was unduly large, wooden poles were placed over stone bases along the middle axis of the room and against its sides. The upright posts would support a ridge pole placed horizontally over the top of the row of upright posts along the middle axis of the room, and purlins were placed over the upright poles set up against the side walls. Or sometimes the upright posts would be tied together. Rafters were then dropped from the ridge pole to the purlins and closely covered with reeds. A thick coat of mud would then be placed over the reeds. Examples of this type of construction were discovered at Byblos.

During the Middle Bronze Age, stone dressing improved tremendously, and in the houses of the rich, the stones were cut into perfect square or rectangular blocks, and the surface was dressed very smooth. The royal palace and the temple of *Baalat Gebal* at Byblos were built of such masonry.

There was no noticeeable change in the architecture of the Late Bronze Age. Good examples of it have been found at Byblos as well as at Ras Shamra, where a palace, temples and houses were found, built of well-dressed squared blocks of masonry.

During the Iron Age, masonry underwent a slight deterioration. The masons of the time became lazy, and instead of dressing the face of the stone entirely smooth, they left a boss on it, and dressed a small margin around three sides only the top and the two sides. This is known as a marginal draft. Examples of this were found at Tyre and Sidon in Phoenicia and at Ahab's palace in Samaria, which was no doubt built by Phoenician masons, or under the supervision of Phoenician masons introduced by Jezebel, Ahab's Tyrian wife. We may also suspect that at least some of the walls of Solomon's temple in Jerusalem, were built of masonry with three marginal drafts, as Hiram the king of Tyre sent masons, carpenters and other artisans to his ally Solomon to build the temple of Jehovah for him.

Whereas the plans of houses did not undergo a radical change during the Iron Age, but remained essentially the same as those of the earlier periods and consisted mainly of a number of rooms ranged along the sides of an open forecourt, a new type of public building made its appearance during the Iron Age, which is now generally known as Bit-hilani, restricted to Temples and Palaces. The Phoenicians no doubt started this type of architecture; although so far no examples of Bit-hilani structures have been

FIGURE 27 *Stele of BAAL,
from Amrit (after* Contenau,
op. cit., p. 1474)

found in Phoenicia, the plan of the Temple in Jerusalem, which was built by Phoenician masons is built on that plan.

The main feature of a Bit-hilani structure is a colonnaded porch. In the case of palaces, the porch was flanked by rooms on either side; doors led from the porch to a large audience hall which in turn gave access to a number of rooms on the three sides. In the case of temples, the porch was not flanked by any room. It led by a single door into the main hall. At the far end of the hall, stood the cella, separated from the main hall by a screen. Within the cella stood the altar.

In important buildings, however, smoothly dressed stones continued to be used.

City-walls during the Iron Age were built of large blocks of squared stones about 2 meters long, 1.50 meters high and at least 1.0 meter deep. Examples of these may still be seen at Aradus and Tyre.

Of the examples of the buildings of the Persian Period, mention may be made of the temple at Amrit and the temple of Eshmun at Sidon. The former consists of a shrine in the middle of an extensive rock cut enclosure. The temple of Eshmun at Sidon, consists of a naos built of large blocks of well-dressed masonry in the middle of a vast enclosure constructed of drafted masonry.

Alexander and the Seleucids introduced Greek methods of construction into Phoenicia. A fourth marginal draft was added to the face of bossed stones, and the walls were built mostly of headers. [1] The three orders of Greek architecture were introduced, the Doric, the Ionic and the Corinthian. Unfortunately most of the Hellenistic structures were destroyed to make room for later buildings, or if they were destroyed by earthquakes or invasions, the material was re-used for more recent buildings. During the Roman Period, there was a great spurt of building activity in Phoenicia, thanks to the orderly government established by the Romans, and the *Pax Romana,* which brought untold wealth to the country in spite of Roman exactions. The Romans introduced their own architecture, which was a modified form of the Hellenistic. Temples were built on the Roman plan, which consisted of a large hall with a raised sanctuary approached by stairs, at the far end of the temple. The sanctuary contained the altar. Outside, the long walls of the temple projected some distance beyond the limit, forming a sort of closed porch in front of the entrance, which was colonnaded. Examples of this may be seen at the temple in Beit Miri, Bziza and Ain Akrit, although strictly speaking these three sites are not in Phoenicia proper. Under the Antonines the plan of Greek temples was followed more faithfully, and peristyle temples, that is temples surrounded by columns on all sides became more fashionable, retaining however the colonnaded porch in front (prostyle in antis), which was a Roman feature. Most of these temples have been destroyed, but examples may be seen outside Phoenicia in Coele-Syria at Baalbek (the temple of Bacchus). The orders of architecture used were the Ionic, as at Bziza, or Corinthian as at Beit Miri and Ain Akrit. Other temples on the coast have been destroyed. We know of their existence from the coins struck during the Roman Period, on which there is often represented a perspective or front view of the Temple. From a coin of the emperor Macrinus (A.D. 217-218) we know of the existence of a peristyle Roman temple at Byblos. This was destroyed by the Crusaders in the twelfth

[1] A header is a long block of stone which crossed the complete width of the wall. A stretcher is a long block, laid parallel to the face of the wall. Generally a stretcher was half as wide as the length of the header so that two stretchers could be laid side by side in the wall between each pair of headers.

century A.D. in order to procure building material for the castle which they built in the same city. Remains of at least two Roman temples, now covered up, were discovered in Beirut. On many of the coins of Beirut struck during the Roman Period, facades of temples, dedicated to Ashtart, Poseidon and Silenus (Marsyas), appear on the reverse. Other temples appear on the coins of Caesarea ad Libanum (Tell Arqa) twenty four kilometres north-east of Tripoli), Botrys (modern Batrun), Dora (modern Tanturah on the coast of Palestine), Ptolemais-Ace (Acre in Palestine), Sidon, Tripolis and Tyre. In addition to the columns, entablatures and friezes which were lavishly decorated with sculpture, the Romans added the arch and the vault, which appear on most coins.

In addition to these temples there are remains of other structures in Phoenicia. At Amrit, there is a fine mausoleum built in two stories of large blocks of smoothly dressed stones, with a moulded cornice on top. It is situated west of the main road to Amrit, and can be approached before the bend in the road from which the Hellenistic thimble-like tombs known as the Maghazel can be seen. At Gabala, modern Jableh, there are the remains of a theatre. At Byblos, a Roman theatre was discovered in the vicinity of the ancient city-gate. It was removed and rebuilt by the excavator near the royal cemetery, close to the sea. The site of the Roman forum at Byblos has been discovered, and some of the columns with their Corinthian capitals have been re-erected. Nearby, the excavator has placed parts of the entablature which surmounted the colonnade.

In Beirut, the *Services des Antiquités* has re-erected part of the colonnade which belonged to the Roman basilica or hall of justice, in front of the National Museum. The basilica was discovered close to the Place de l'Étoile a few years ago.

The Romans also introduced polychrome mosaic floors into Phoenicia. Examples of these were found at Tyre, Ṣidon, Beirut and other places in Phoenicia.

During the Byzantine Period many Christian churches were erected in the country. These churches have either been rebuilt several times, or destroyed and abandoned, and so far as the present writer is aware there is no church in Phoenicia which is still in use that goes back to the Byzantine Period. The plan of a Byzantine church was copied from that of the Roman basilica

or Hall of Justice. Most of them were orientated east-west. In size
the churches varied with the size of the city or village in which
they were built. Generally, the church was built along one side
of a square colonnaded atrium or forecourt. The church itself
consisted of a long hall, the nave with a round apse for the clergy
and choir at the east end. There were two narrow aisles on either
side of the central nave separated from it by a colonnade. Some
churches had a narrow vestibule, the narthex, just inside the door
which was on the west, where the catecumens, or unbatized
converts stood during the service. The chancel was at the east
end of the church and spread over the apse and part of the nave.
It was separated from the nave by a marble screen about a metre
high. The altar was placed in the middle of the apse. At the end
of the north aisle, in some churches there was a prothesis, where
the sacrament was prepared, while at the east end of the south
aisle, there was a diakonikon where the deacons officiated during
the less important services. If the church possessed the relics of a
saint, they were generally placed in a stone casket under the altar.
Around the round wall of the apse, there were seats for the bishop
and priests.

The floors of Byzantine churches were covered with a polychrome mosaic pavement. This followed a more or less stereotyped
pattern. The narthex generally had a white surround, a border
of black lines, and a field decorated with a scale pattern in red
and black over a white background. The floor of the church
usually had a white surround, a guilloche or interlacing border
in black, red and white enclosed within rows of black tesserae
and a field consisting of a vase at the west end of the nave from
which vine branches sprout and form circular medallions, spreading
over the entire floor of the nave; in each medallion there was an
animal or a bird, or scenes from daily life. As many as fifteen colours
may have been used including black, white, red, pink, brown and
green in various shades. Sometimes a dedicatory inscription would
be laid in mosaics either in front of the chancel or in the surround
at the west end of the church just inside the entrance. The floor
of the apse and the lateral aisles generally consisted of a white
background decorated with red and white sprigs or arrow-like
ornaments. A ruined Byzantine church, with a mosaic pavement
was discovered by the British Army in 1918 in Ras Beirut. The

mosaic pavement was removed and relaid in the Museum of the American University of Beirut. The masonry of Byzantine buildings was considerably smaller than that of Roman masonry, but the Phoenicians during the Byzantine Period continued to use the Roman orders of architecture, principally the Corinthian.

CHAPTER V
Present Monuments in Phoenicia

It now remains to single out the important monuments of Phoenicia, and describe those among them that have not received sufficient attention in the foregoing pages. The writer will start with Ras Shamra in the north and proceed as far as Dora in the south.

Ras Shamra, ancient Ugarit, is situated about twelve kilometres north of Lattaqia. Dr. Schaeffer started excavating the site in 1929, and followed it up by ten other field campaigns when World War II put a stop to the excavation for a period of twelve years. In 1951 Dr. Schaeffer resumed the excavations which have been followed up every autumn ever since. Dr. Schaeffer uncovered a large part of the city-walls, which were defended by towers all having battered walls. [1] The city gate was built of corbelled stones which formed an inverted angle, like the tombs at Mycenae. Inside the city-walls, a large palace, or rather several palaces of various dates, were discovered superimposed one on top of the other. Also there were several temples, houses and tombs. A large amount of pottery was discovered in the palace, in the houses, and in the temples and the tombs which belong to the Late Bronze Age. In a small area, Dr. Schaeffer made a deep sounding in which he found five successive occupation levels, the earliest of which is Neolithic in age followed by the Chalcolithic (Level IV), Early Bronze (Level III), Middle Bronze (Level II) and Late Bronze Age (Level I) levels, when Ugarit was destroyed by the "People of the Sea" (the Aegeans) about 1194 B.C. and never rose again. The objects discovered at Ras Shamra include the tablets in King Niqmad's library which have already been described, and which are now partly in the Louvre, partly in the Aleppo Museum and partly in the National Museum at Damascus. Ivory carvings, a gold patera, weapons, jewellery and other works of art were also discovered and may be inspected in any of the three museums aforementioned.

[1] Battered walls are walls built at a slope.

At Aradus, nothing can be seen except the Phoenician city-walls. The monuments of Amrit have already been mentioned. Recently M. Maurice Dunand, of Byblos fame, has opened up excavations on the ancient city site, and has made important discoveries.

Ever since that landslide of 1922 which revealed the tomb of Ipshemuabi, the site of Byblos has been under systematic excavation under the auspices of the Lebanese Government. The excavations were opened by M. P. Montet, who supervized four campaigns from 1921-1924, and continued by M. Maurice Dunand who except for a short interruption on account of the World War of 1939-1945, is still proceeding with the excavations. The discoveries were sensational. Apart from the royal cemetery which was discovered, and which revealed such a rich variety of examples of Phoenician art, the earliest Phoenician inscription in the cursive alphabet known so far was discovered on the sarcophagus of Ahiram. A cross-section of Phoenician culture and civilization from the Neolithic Period to the Roman Period was obtained from the excavation of this single site. The city-walls, the palaces, the temples, the Forum and the theatre have already been described. The small objects from Byblos which were discovered in these various buildings and in foundation deposits are now in the National Museum in Beirut.

In recent years, many chance discoveries have been made in Beirut of remains that go back to the fifteenth century B.C. thus confirming the evidence given in the Tell el-Amarna letters as to the existence of Beirut during the Late Bronze Age. Many of the Roman buildings in Beirut, discovered over a long period of time, have recently been published by the *Services des Antiquités du Liban* in a brochure which gives one a glimpse of the important place the city held during the Roman Period. One cannot discuss Beirut without mentioning the Dog River, with its vista across the ages in the form of stelae carved out of the living rock on its south bank such as the stele of Ramses II recording his defeat of Mutallu, king of the Hittites, and next to it, by an irony of fate, the stele of Esarhaddon, king of Assyria recording his subjugation of Egypt. There are many other stelae there, too numerous to describe in a book of this size.

At Sidon, there is the temple of Eshmun, and close-by at

FIGURE 28   *Stele of Yahumelek (after* Contenau, *op. cit., p. 1475)*

Kafr Jarra, a cemetery was discovered ranging in date from the nineteenth century B.C. to the twelfth. At the rival city of Tyre, the *Services des Antiquités du Liban* has been conducting excavations for some years under the able direction of Emir Maurice Chehab, Director-General of Antiquities. A Roman forum and basilica have been discovered, as well as an assembly hall where the town councillors used to meet. Earlier walls belonging to the Persian Period and the Iron Age are in process of being uncovered, besides a very fine sarcophagus of the Hellenistic Period, carved with a shell pattern. At the beginning of the causeway built by Alexander the Great, a Roman cemetery containing a number of marble sarcophagi has been exposed. In the sea south and west of Tyre, one may still see the foundations of temples, built in the sea, and probably dedicated to Neptune. At Tell er-Rashidiyeh, Palaeatyrus, or Continental Tyre, several tombs belonging to the Early and Middle Iron Age have come to light. Phoenician Acre has been completely obliterated by age, but Phoenician Haifa was excavated by the Department of Antiquities in Palestine. It was so thoroughly excavated that it was wiped off the map. City-walls, temples and other buildings were discovered, ranging from the Late Bronze Age to the Hellenistic Period. Phoenician pottery predominated during the Iron Age. At Athlit, a Phoenician cemetery was discovered belonging to the Middle Iron Age and Persian Periods.

The great Phoenician cities of Sidon and Tyre have in actual fact been disappointing. For one thing it is well nigh impossible to excavate an inhabited city, and for another, the two cities have undergone such devastating destruction in the fourth century B.C. that the libraries and other important and valuable material for the study of the history and culture of Phoenicia have been irretrievably lost.

The antiquities of Phoenicia are dispersed in the various museums of the world but, since the creation of the *Services des Antiquités du Liban* in 1920, only a small number of antiquities have filtered out of the country. These mainly constitute the share of excavators from the finds. But the bulk of the artistic heritage of Phoenicia is now concentrated in the Beirut National Museum, which includes the entire treasures from Byblos, as well as the stone monuments discovered there, the anthropomorphic sarcophagi bequeathed by the late Dr. Ford to the Lebanese Government, the sarcophagus of Ahiram, the sarcophagus from Sidon decorated with the representation of a galley, examples of Hellenistic and Roman sculpture executed in Phoenicia, the painted Hellenistic tomb from Bramieh near Sidon, Phoenician glass, pottery, weapons and numerous other artefacts.

Ras Shamra, Aradus, Marathus and Simyra now fall outside Lebanon in the neighbouring country of Syria, hence all ancient objects of art found in these sites are housed either in the Museum of Aleppo, or in the National Museum at Damascus. Many of the tablets from Ras Shamra and a great number of pots are in Aleppo. The carved ivories discovered in 1952 and some tablets are in Damascus.

In 1860 a French expedition was sent to Phoenicia and Syria to explore the country scientifically. The great French *savant*, Ernest Renan was placed in charge. Together with a number of assistants, he explored the regions of Aradus, Byblos, Sidon and Tyre. During the course of their researches they discovered many monuments. There being no Department of Antiquities in Lebanon at the time to look after the precious objects discovered, the antiquities were taken either to the Louvre Museum or to the museum at Constantinople. As a result of this and later expeditions both

French and Turkish, there is a large collection of valuable antiquities from Phoenicia in the Louvre and another important collection in Constantinople.

Among the most important objects in the Louvre is the sarcophagus of Eshmunazar discovered near Sidon which has already been mentioned. To this we now add the stele of Baal of the Thunderbolt from Ras Shamra, the stele of Yahumelek, king of Byblos, the ivory plaque with the Mycenaean deity from Ras Shamra, the stele of Baal from Amrit, the stele from Umm el Amad south of Tyre, numerous figurines in bronze and terra cotta, and numerous other objects in bronze, glass and pottery. Besides a large variety of small objects, some of extreme beauty and delicacy, the greatest finds of Sidon are kept in Constantinople. They include the sarcophagus of Tabnit, the so-called Alexander sarcophagus, the sarcophagi of the Satrap, the Lycian and the Weepers. It would be a forlorn and idle hope to wish that these might one day return to their home of origin and the mother country that yearns for them.

CHAPTER VI

Conclusion

One of the failings of humanity is to judge the relative importance of any country by its territorial size, and by its ability to extend its dominion over neighbouring countries, the total area of which may be considerably larger than its own. Phoenicia and the Phoenicians, according to this verdict would not constitute a great country or a great nation. Yet this narrow strip of country stretching along the eastern littoral of the Mediterranean played a great role in the ancient history of the world. It did not seek, it could not seek territorial expansion, but it held for a period of four centuries and a half, complete mastery of the Mediterranean, and for a period of three centuries was mistress of the Aegean as well. It was the unrivalled and undisputed trading nation between east and west. It carried to the West, as represented by the Greeks, the products of the East and carried to the East the products of the West. It developed the alphabet, thus rendering a great and abiding service to humanity. For that alone, if for nothing else, the Phoenicians must be classed among the great nations of the world. In seamanship, it made use of the stars as a guide in navigation, a knowledge which it inherited from the astronomers of Babylonia, and passed on to the Greeks, and from them to the Romans and thereby revolutionized navigation, and sailed on hitherto uncharted seas. It taught the West accounting and book-keeping which again it learnt from Babylonia and passed on to the West. It invented glass, both moulded, which it retained as a monopoly, and blown glass which it passed on to Gaul and Italy in the west. That the Phoenicians were great traders of merchandize is fully realized and appreciated but, while they were carrying on this trade, they also disseminated knowledge and culture. They did not only barter goods for goods, to their great profit and gain, but they also bartered the ideas of the east for those of the west to the benefit not only of the Phoenicians, but for the benefit of mankind at large. Their role in propagating the lore and culture of the east in the west and vice-versa cannot be over-emphasized. Greek art and culture found its way into the east before Alexander set his foot across the Dardanelles. Witness the Greek Attic vases of the sixth and fifth centuries B.C. in Phoenicia and the Near East. They were not brought in Greek vessels to these parts. Witness the sculpture of the Phoenicians of the Persian Period. Surely a nation which held sway over the wide expanse of the Mediterranean for four and a half centuries is not a whit inferior to the land empires of Egypt, of the Hittites or of Assyria. Yet the contributions of the Phoenicians to world civilization and humanity should not be judged by the small size of their country or the extent of their hegemony but by the real and lasting value of the contributions themselves. The Phoenicians not only made original contributions, which have proved to be of great service to mankind but also, thanks to their constant peregrinations over the Mediterranean during the Golden Age of Phoenicia and later, they propagated their own contributions to culture as well as those of their neighbours, all over the ancient world. The Phoenicians were carriers of ideas as well as carriers of goods, and their peregrinations accelerated the tempo of the progress of culture and civilization in the ancient world.

In a previous chapter we have ventured to express some views concerning the origin of the real Phoenicians, the Phoenicians of the Golden Age, as opposed to the proto-Phoenician Canaanites who dwelt on the Phoenician coast from the twenty-second century B.C. to the twelfth, and who did not venture to create a thalassocracy over the high seas. This theory, although arrived at by the present writer independently, suggested itself to the author soon after taking charge of the Museum of the American University of Beirut. In the course of his research on this subject, the author found that a precisely similar idea had occurred to a predecessor in the same office. Sir Leonard Woolley, in an article entitled *La Phénicie et les Peuples Egéens* came to the same conclusion, basing his views on the close similarity of the pottery of the Early Iron Age in Phoenicia with that of the previous period, the Late Bronze Age, in Mycenae and Cyprus, and obviously developing from it, when the pottery of the hinterland was developing on totally different lines. Sir Leonard also attributed the close and amicable relations prevailing between the Aegeans of Cyprus and the Phoenicians as arising out of the blood relationship of the rulers of the two countries. The facts of the case may be summarized as follows: We know from contemporary documents that large forces of Aegeans, or "People of the Sea" as they were called in contemporary documents, attacked the Hittite Empire and the coast of Phoenicia and Palestine about 1194 B.C. They were sufficiently strong to destroy the powerful Hittite Empire and descend on Ras Shamra, Aradus, and Simyra and destroy them in their stride. Another wave, coming from the south, was allowed to settle in Palestine, attack Tyre and Sidon and sack them, although they had previously been defeated by Ramses III at Pelusium. There is no evidence that the Aegeans or "People of the Sea" were ever expelled from the country or left it of their own accord; but there is strong evidence that they settled and entrenched themselves securely on the coast of Phoenicia. Wenamon, the Egyptian emissary, found them at Dora (modern Tanturah) and Byblos in the eleventh century B.C. The Aegeans who settled in Phoenicia established trading factories in Cyprus, and their culture followed the pattern of Cyprus so closely that the two became indistinguishable. The Aegean hegemony over the seas came to an end with the Dorian invasion of Greece, and into the gap thus left, the Phoenicians stepped without opposition from anyone. They held that thalassocracy for four hundred and fifty years. Would it be too much, in view of all this evidence, to conclude that this great sea-power resulted from the fusion of the proto-Phoenician Canaanites and the Aegeans or "People of the Sea"? We think not.

Before we end this discussion, it would be well to take another important factor into consideration. M. Raymond Weill has demonstrated that the Egyptians had a general term to designate Syria, Crete and the entire basin of the Eastern Mediterranean as *Keftiu* in the fifteenth century B.C. The Early Hellenes gave the name Phoenicia to precisely the same area but this name was later restricted to the coast of Syria. M. Weill goes on to explain that this is exactly the opposite of the normal process where the name of a small area tends with time rather to embrace a much larger area. For example Philistia was originally the name of strip of land in the Holy Land between Jaffa in the north and Gaza in the south, with the foothills of Judaea forming its eastern boundary. In process of time, the name Palestine came to embrace the entire country. M. Weill then continues to say "this is a less explicable phenomenon." May we suggest that by *Keftiu* the Egyptians meant the Aegean World, that the primitive Hellenes gave the term Phoenician to precisely the same area, and that when the Aegeans were ousted from Crete and the Aegean world and settled in Phoenicia, the name Phoenicians followed them, and the fact that Phoenicia was inhabited originally by the proto-Phoenician Canaanites only, was forgotten.

This view will explain many facts which seem otherwise inexplicable. The Phoenicians were able quickly to take to the sea, and fill the gaps left by the Aegeans. They were able to sail in uncharted seas such as the African Coast from the Pillars of Hercules to the Isthmus of Suez as well as in the Aegean basin, because the first generation of them, and perhaps even the second still remembered every cove and harbour on the Aegean shore. Although the Aegeans had a lot to teach the original inhabitants in seamanship they also had a lot to learn from them.

Excavations have shown that the Aegeans of Crete extracted the purple dye from the murex shell; vast quantities of empty shells can still be seen on the coast of Crete. We have seen that the extraction of the purple dye from the murex shell was one of the chief industries of Phoenicia. Is it too much to suppose that the Aegeans brought to Phoenicia their lore of seamanship, their methods of extracting the purple dye from the murex shell, and their pottery-making techniques and designs? The evidence appears weighty in favour of a reply in the affirmative.

In the process of a very short time the role of master (Aegean) and subject (proto-Phoenician Canaanite) disappeared, and the newcomers with their lore and culture, were assimilated and absorbed by the original inhabitants. The resulting nation, the Phoenician, came into being. Such a fusion of races generally gives birth to a nation which outstrips its parents in intelligence, and energy, and this goes a long way to explain the greatness to which Phoenicia rose during the twelfth to eighth centuries B.C.

However the writer does not wish to ignore the external circumstances which also added their quota to being about the greatness of the Phoenicians. One of these was the collapse of the Achaean thalassocracy in the Aegean thanks to the Dorian invasion. However, there were other factors. After the reign of Ramses III, the Empire of Egypt collapsed on account of internal disorder and external invasion. Babylonia and Assyria were occupied in a tug-of-war struggle for supremacy in the Land of the Two Rivers. The Hittite Empire was no more. Under Tiglath Pileser I (1110-1076 B.C.) Assyria did manage to carve out an empire stretching from the Black Sea to the Persian Gulf and from the Mediterranean to the Zagros Mountains, but this empire was of short duration, and collapsed with the death of its founder. His successors were apathetic and allowed the empire to disintegrate quickly and be forgotten. The time was ripe for Phoenicia and the small neighbouring countries of the Israelites, the Arameans of Damascus, the Moabites and Edomites of Trans-Jordan to enjoy a period of independence and indulge in petty warfare of their own. As the Phoenicians' main interest was the sea, they did not interfere in the struggle between the petty states of the hinterland and went ahead to claim the sea as their own, without fear of attack from Egypt, Hatti, Babylonia or Assyria. The result of their endeavour was a great boon to mankind. It was contact with the Orient through the Phoenicians that brought about the civilization and culture of Greece, the fountain head of our political, social and cultural institutions. Greece and Greek culture owe a tremendous debt to Phoenicia, a debt which is freely admitted by the Greeks themselves, by no less a person than the Father of History, Herodotus; and the testimony of an enemy and a rival is the greatest recognition of a man's or nation's ability, capacity and greatness.

Bibliography

Many books and articles were consulted by the author, which if added here, would cover a large number of pages. Most of these books and articles appear in the bibliographies of the books listed below. The author appends here a list of the most important books consulted.

W.F. ALBRIGHT: *Archaeology of Palestine.*

G. CONTENEAU: *La Civilisation Phénicienne*; contains an excellent bibliography.

G. CONTENEAU: *Manuel d'Archéologie Orientale*, Tomes I-IV.

O'LEARY: *Arabia before Muhammad.*

Encyclopaedia Britannica: Article on Phoenicia by G.A. COOKE.

P. MONTET: *Byblos et L'Egypte.*

M. DUNAND: *Fouilles de Byblos*, Vols. I and II.

G. CONTENEAU: *Mission Archéologique à Sidon* 1914, *Deuxième Mission Archéologique à Sidon* 1920.

Th. REINACH et HAMDY Bey: *Une Nécropole à Sidon.*

J.A. WILSON: *The Megiddo Ivories.*

H.R. HALL: *Ancient History of the Near East.*

CARY: *History of Rome.*

BURY: *History of Greece.*

WOOLLEY: *A Forgotten Kingdom.*

WOOLLEY: Article in Syria, Vol. II. — *La Phénicie et les Peuples Egéens.*

SCHAEFFER: *Stratigraphie Comparée et Chronologie de l'Asie Occidentale.*

SCHAEFFER: *Ugaritica I — Ugaritica II — Ugaritica III.*

OBERMANN: *Ugaritic Mythology.*

CROWFOOT: *The Samaria Ivories.*

BREASTED: *History of Egypt.*

H.L. LORIMER: *Homer and the Monuments.*

V. BERARD: *Les Phéniciens et l'Odyssée.*

The Old Testament.

G.F. HILL: *Catalogue of the Greek coins of Phoenicia in the British Museum.*

ROUVIER: *Numismatique des Villes de la Phénicie.*

NEWELL: *Coins of Eastern Dynasts.*

P. DHORME: *Les Achéens dans les Textes de Boghaz-Keni.*

TH. GASTER: *The Oldest Stories in the World.*

Phoenicia and the Phoenicians

M. CHEHAB: *Article in Bulletin du Musée de Beyrouth.*
HERODOTUS: *History*, Books I-IV.
PLUTARCH: *Lives.*
HOMER: *Iliad and Odyssey.*
VERGIL: *Aeneid.*
CAMBRIDGE: *Ancient History.*

Index

119

Index